DIGITA

Digital Humanism is the book we have been waiting for. Techno gurus, post-humanists, environmentalists, post-colonialists and post-structuralists will have you believe that humanist ethics is no longer relevant to the contemporary world. Yet, as this book demonstrates unflinchingly, never before has humanism been so relevant to the contemporary period. Humanism offers a philosophical and ethical reflection on the recklessness and havoc wrought by human choices and constitutes an attempt to formulate the conditions for a hospitable social world. *Digital Humanism* refuses to transform humans into machines and to think of machines as humans. This is why this book is such an important and timely intervention.

– *Eva Illouz, Directrice d'Etudes, École des hautes études en sciences sociales (EHESS), France*

DIGITAL HUMANISM

A Philosophy for 21st Century Digital Society

BY

CHRISTIAN FUCHS
Paderborn University, Germany

United Kingdom – North America – Japan – India
Malaysia – China

Emerald Publishing Limited
Howard House, Wagon Lane, Bingley BD16 1WA, UK

First edition 2022

British Library Cataloguing in Publication Data
A catalogue record for this book is available from the British Library

ISBN: 978-1-80382-422-2 (Print)
ISBN: 978-1-80382-419-2 (Online)
ISBN: 978-1-80382-421-5 (Epub)

CONTENTS

LIST OF TABLES AND FIGURES

1

INTRODUCTION

Digital Humanism is a contribution to the moral philosophy of digital society. It introduces the approach of Digital Humanism and asks: Why is Humanist philosophy important in the contemporary digital age? How can Humanism help us to critically understand how digital technologies shape society and humanity? What kind of Humanism do we need to make sense of digitalisation in society? This book contributes to the renewal of Humanist philosophy in the digital age.

Our contemporary global digital society is not a good place to live in. Authoritarianism and nationalism are major forces in many parts of the world. Authoritarianism and hatred are constantly circulating their ideologies on the Internet and via social media. Along with them, there is an attack on truth and quality media. We have experienced how false news have influenced election results and dominate everyday politics. There is talk of post-truth politics. Too many people distrust the very ideas of facts, truth, experts and research. They believe that truth is what they find emotionally comforting and ideologically acceptable. Algorithms create and manage attention and visibility on the Internet that shape politics. In algorithmic politics, it has become intransparent if a certain piece of information that circulates online has been created by a human being or a robot. Robots and Artificial Intelligence (AI) shape and influence the worlds of work, consumption, leisure, decision-making, transportation, manufacturing, healthcare, education, news and entertainment. Many humans wonder if human autonomy and decision-making can and will be replaced by AI-powered robots. Digital surveillance is ubiquitous. It is used by both governments and capitalist companies as means of control. We have experienced the demise of the public sphere in the digital age. News and information have to be short, superficial and entertaining in order to reach a significant audience. The public sphere is fragmented into micro-publics, filter bubbles and echo chambers so that humans are unable to talk to each other. Right-wing extremists steer hatred online against migrants, refugees, feminists, socialists, liberals, experts and quality media. The public sphere is highly polarised. As a consequence, many humans tend to think of other humans mainly in terms of friends and enemies. Digital technologies also shape warfare. Digital warfare has extended and intensified the destructive capacities of military technologies. Massive amounts of electronic waste and the powering of digital technologies by fossil fuel–based energy and nuclear energy has contributed to the environmental crisis and environmental risks. The COVID-19 pandemic has shown the vulnerability of humanity to viruses and health crises. In the pandemic, humans were forced to re-organise their lives online in order to survive, which created new inequalities and problems.

Humanity and society are in a major crisis. Digitalisation mediates the crisis of humanity and society. How will society look in 10, 20 and 50 years from now? Will society and humanity still exist? Or will they have come to an end? Will society have been destroyed by wars, environmental disasters and escalating crises? Will new fascisms have emerged that enslave humanity? Will we live in barbarity where the rich rule humanity and kill and treat others at will? Or will an alternative social order that guarantees peace, wealth, happiness, justice, freedom, equality and sustainability for all have emerged? We do not know the answer to these questions, yet it is important that we think about what has brought humanity into the situation it is in now and what ways there are out of the crisis of humanity.

Capitalism is based on an antagonism between individual freedom and social justice. The Enlightenment and the French Revolution advanced the idea of human rights, which include political rights and the right of individuals to own as much property and capital as they can accumulate. Capitalist ownership replaced feudal lordship. Newly established freedoms also established new forms of domination such as wage-labour and capitalist monopolies. The individual freedom of ownership undermines the Enlightenment's promise to realise equality and solidarity as universal rights. Capitalist society undermines social freedom. Capitalist society is based on what the critical theorists Max Horkheimer and Adorno term the dialectic of Enlightenment. Capitalism entails the tendency of the 'self-destruction of enlightenment' (Horkheimer and Adorno 2002, xvi) so that there is the potential for 'the reversion of enlightened civilization to barbarism' (xix).

Capitalism's 'dialectics of enlightenment' can reach 'the point where this dialectics terminates in the abolition of reason' (Adorno 1973/2004, 385) and results in 'outbursts of the irrational' (Adorno 2006, 15), and 'a destruction of rational thought, so that what is left at the end of this process lends itself all too readily to irrationalism and counter-Enlightenment' (Adorno 2019, 121).

Capitalism has the potential to produce Auschwitz. Auschwitz shows that the 'antireason of totalitarian capitalism [...] tends toward the extermination of humanity' (Horkheimer and Adorno 2002, 43). Capitalism promises to advance Humanism but at the same time has destructive and fascist potentials. Given that capitalism promises Humanism that it actually often subverts, we should not discard Humanism, modernity and universalism – as Postmodernists have done – but argue and struggle for overcoming their particularistic character and for universalising Humanism, modernity and universalism so that everyone benefits. Adorno writes in this context that the dialectic of Enlightenment does not imply the need to abolish the Enlightenment, but rather to fully realise it: 'the wounds which enlightenment has left behind' are 'the moments where enlightenment itself betrays its own imperfect character and reveals that it is actually not yet enlightened enough. And it is only by pursuing the principle of enlightenment through to the end that these wounds may perhaps be healed' (Adorno 2017, 188).

Capitalist production is not simply an economic model, it is a political economy. This means that class struggles, laws and policies shape the capitalist economy's specific character and the distribution of power in it. How much (in)equality and social (in)justice exists is a political economy question.

In the 1970s, the model of neoliberal capitalism emerged that became a global political economy. It is based on an empowerment of property owners, capital, finance capital, transnational corporations vis-à-vis workers, the poor, the unemployed and trade unions. Some of its features include the privatisation and commodification of public services and common goods, transnational corporations' global outsourcing of labour, the formation of precarious labour, the creation of digital capital, the financialisation of the economy, high-risk financial derivatives and low taxes for corporations and the rich. Neoliberalism is accumulation by dispossession (Harvey 2003):

> *Accumulation by dispossession became increasingly more salient after 1973, in part as compensation for the chronic problems of overaccumulation arising within expanded reproduction. The primary vehicle for this development was financialization [...] But the opening up of new territories to capitalist development and to capitalistic forms of market behaviour also played a role, as did the primitive accumulations accomplished in those countries (such as South Korea, Taiwan, and now, even more dramatically, China) that sought to insert themselves into global capitalism as active players. For all of this to occur required not only financialization and freer trade, but a radically different approach to how state power, always a major player in accumulation by dispossession, should be deployed. The rise of neo-liberal theory and its associated politics of privatization symbolized much of what this shift was about.*
>
> (Harvey 2003, 156)

Neoliberalism exacerbated socio-economic inequalities so that the rich and corporations controlled a larger and increasing share of global wealth and workers and others a smaller and shrinking share. In neoliberalism, the antagonism between individual private capital and social justice reached new heights. Precarious life, precarious labour and the unequal distribution of wealth significantly increased (Piketty 2014). Capital colonised ever larger parts and realms of life. Capitalist profit interests were put over human interests and human beings. The antagonisms between capital and labour, austerity and precarity, profits and humans deepened.

Fig. 1.1 shows the development of the average adjusted wage share for 21 countries. The wage share is the share of total wages in the gross domestic product. I used the data for all countries for which data were available. The wage share shows the economic power of labour vis-à-vis capital. A higher wage share means that the share of capital in the GDP is lower and vice versa. The wage share was available for these countries on an annual basis. I calculated the average of all countries for each year.

Between 1960 and the middle of the 1970s, the wage share was rising, which reflects the importance of welfare states, union power, and the role of working-class struggles. In 1975, the average wage share reached a height of 64.1%. The subsequent rise of neoliberalism brought wage-repression and the redistribution of income from labour to capital with it. In the year 2000, the average wage share dropped to 55.2%. In 2022, it stood with 53.1% at the lowest level in the analysis period that covers 62 years. 'The labour income share has displayed a downward trend in many economies, both developed and developing, since the 1980s, with a corresponding rise in the profit share. The proximate cause has been wage repression, due to the weakening of labour market institutions, which has prevented wages from keeping pace with increases in productivity and, in many cases, the cost of living' (UNCTAD 2020, 65).

Table 1.1 shows data for the development of the wage share at the global level and at various regional and organisational levels. In the time period covered, the wage share either stayed very low (Africa, Latin America) or it further dropped. At the world level, it dropped from 53.7% in 2004 to 51.4% in 2017.

Capitalism is crisis-ridden. In 2008, the antagonisms of neoliberal capitalism exploded into a new world economic

Fig. 1.1. The Development of the Average Adjusted Wage Share in 21 Countries. Countries: Australia, Austria, Belgium, Canada, Denmark, Finland, France, Germany, Greece, Iceland, Ireland, Italy, Japan, Luxembourg, Netherlands, Norway, Portugal, Spain, Sweden, United Kingdom, USA.

Table 1.1. Global and Regional Data for the Development of the Wage Share as Percent of GDP, Data Source: International Labour Organisation.

	World	Africa	Latin America and Caribbean	North America	Asia and the Pacific	Europe and Central Asia	EU28	G20	ASEAN	BRICS
2004	53.7	47.1	48.4	61.7	50.5	56.7	59.4	55.6	41.9	53.2
2005	53	46.4	48.3	60.7	50.1	56.2	59.2	54.8	41.8	52.2
2006	52.5	46.2	48.2	60.6	49.4	55.8	58.8	54.3	41.8	51.3
2007	52.3	45.7	47.6	60.9	48.8	55.9	58.9	54	41.8	50.7
2008	52.6	45.2	48.2	61.1	50	56.3	59.1	54.4	42.9	52.2
2009	53.5	46.1	50.4	60.5	50.5	58.2	60.4	55.2	43.4	53.5
2010	52.2	45.7	49	59.4	49.1	57	59.8	53.9	42	51.8
2011	51.5	46.7	49.3	59.2	49	55.2	58.8	53.1	41.8	50.6
2012	51.5	46.6	49.8	59.3	49	55.3	58.9	53.1	41.5	50.7
2013	51.5	47.2	50.5	58.8	49.1	55.3	58.5	53.1	41.5	51.5
2014	51.7	47.5	50.8	58.7	49.4	55.3	58.4	53.2	41.2	51.9
2015	51.8	47.9	51.1	59.3	49.3	54.8	57.8	53.3	40.6	52
2016	51.7	47.5	51	59.2	49.2	55	57.9	53.3	40.5	51.9
2017	51.4	47.4	50.5	58.8	49	54.6	57.6	52.9	40.1	51.6

crisis. The predominant reaction of politics was not a U-turn but more of the same, an intensification of neoliberalism that became known as austerity politics. Capital was made fit again at the expense of workers and human interests. Neoliberalism weakened the organised labour movement and its capacity to engage in class struggles. The Left was weakened by constant anti-socialist attacks. More and more humans had enough. They were searching for alternatives. Right-wing authoritarian forces were mobilised by steering resentments against minorities and using the friend/enemy ideology. Trump, Brexit and the rise of right-wing authoritarian forces that threaten democracy were the consequence. Neoliberalism's negative dialectic exploded into the rise of new nationalisms, right-wing authoritarianism, racism and new fascisms that distract attention of the working class from the actual capitalist causes of social misery.

Whereas in capitalism, in general, capital dominates over humans, an antagonism which was intensified in neoliberal capitalism, a new form of authoritarian capitalism, has emerged where digital capital dominates over humans and human interests. Digital capital, as organised in the form of the hardware of the software industry, big data, social media, targeted advertising, cloud computing, the Internet of Things, algorithms, surveillance systems and more, now dominates daily life. This has given rise to an increase in nationalistic, racist and fascist collectives, authoritarian structures, polarised and fragmented publics; as well as structures of distrust into experts, science, education and quality news. The reality of neoliberal capitalism has resulted in threats to democracy and the rise of new forms of anti-Humanism. Today, society is at a crossroads between Humanism and barbarism. Only if a broad coalition of progressive forces opposed to fascism and destruction unites and creates a front that struggles for Humanism, can the descent into barbarism be circumvented.

Humanism is an important practical force for saving humanity today from descent into barbarism.

This book is a contribution to the moral philosophy of digital society. It asks: How can Humanism help us to critically understand how digital technologies shape society and humanity?

For providing an answer to this overarching question, the book introduces the approach of Digital Humanism. It provides a general introduction to Digital Humanism and advocates a particular version of Digital Humanism that I call Radical Digital Humanism. *Digital Humanism* provides an introduction to Humanism in the digital age. It analyses what decolonisation of academia and the study of the digital, media and communication means; what the roles are of robots, automation and AI in digital capitalism; and how the communication of death and dying has been mediated by digital technologies, capitalist necropower and digital capitalism. Organised in the form of six chapters, an introduction, and a conclusion, the main question is subdivided into further questions this book deals with:

- Chapter 2: What is Humanism?
- Chapter 3: What is Digital Humanism?
- Chapter 4: What does it mean to decolonise academia and the study of media, communication and the digital? How can academia be transformed in progressive ways?
- Chapter 5: How can we understand and theorise the impacts of robots and AI on everyday life based on Radical Humanism?
- Chapter 6: How do the AI strategies of the EU, the United States under Donald Trump and China look like?
- Chapter 7: What is the role of the communication of death and dying in capitalist society? How has communication

with dying loved ones changed in the COVID-19 pandemic? What roles have digital technologies and capitalism played in this context?

Chapter 2's title is 'What is Humanism?'. The chapter discusses definitions of Humanism. It synthesises such definitions in order to provide a philosophical understanding of Humanism. This understanding has epistemological, ontological and axiological dimensions. The chapter points out that Humanism is transcultural. Common objections to Humanism are discussed by engaging with the works of the historian Yuval Noah Harari. Based on the general understanding of Humanism, the approach of Radical Humanism is introduced. Radical Humanism is a particular form of Humanism. Its epistemological, ontological and axiological aspects are outlined. The chapter discusses four examples approaches of Radical Humanism (Karl Marx, Erich Fromm, Wang Ruoshui, David Harvey).

Chapter 3's title is 'What is Digital Humanism?'. It deals with the question: What is Digital Humanism? It argues that Digital Humanism is a philosophy suited for the analysis of the digital age that has specific epistemological, ontological and axiological dimensions. It also introduces a specific version of Digital Humanism, namely Radical Digital Humanism. It argues that we need to advance the co-operation of all Humanisms in order circumvent the rise of new fascisms in the digital age. The chapter also discusses and responds to objections to Digital Humanism.

Chapter 4's title is 'Decolonising Academia: A Radical Humanist Perspective'. It reflects on calls for and processes of the decolonisation of the academic field of Media and Communication Studies. It asks: What does it mean to decolonise academia and the study of media, communication and the digital? How can academia be transformed in progressive ways? The chapter takes a Radical Humanist and Political Economy perspective on decolonisation, which means that it is interested in how capitalism, power and material aspects of academia such as resources, money, infrastructures, time, space, working conditions and social relations of production shape the possibilities and realities of research and teaching. Chapter 4 stresses the importance of defining (neo-)colonialism as foundation of debates about decolonisation and engages with theoretical foundations and definitions of (neo-)colonisation. It identifies how material forces and political economy shape and negatively impede on the university and academic knowledge production. The chapter provides perspectives for concrete steps that can and should be taken for overcoming the capitalist and colonised university and creating the public interest and commons-oriented university and academic system.

Chapter 5's title is 'Robots and Artificial Intelligence (AI) in Digital Capitalism'. The chapter asks: How can we understand and theorise the impacts of robots and AI on everyday life based on Radical Humanism? How can Lefebvre's ideas be used to reveal the ideological character of contemporary accounts of the impacts of robots and AI on society? It engages with rather unknown works of the Radical Humanist Henri Lefebvre on the sociology and philosophy of technology such as *Vers le cybernanthrope* (*Towards the Cybernanthrope*). Foundations of a Lefebvrian, dialectical, Radical Humanist approach to the sociology and philosophy of technology are presented. The chapter introduces Lefebvre's notion of the cybernanthrope and sets it in relation to robots and AI in contemporary society. Based on Lefebvre's critique of the cybernanthrope, Chapter 5 develops foundations of the ideology critique of robots and AI in digital capitalism. It discusses examples of technological deterministic and social constructivist thought in the context of robotics, AI and cyborgs and argues for an alternative, Lefebvrian, dialectical approach. The chapter situates Humanism in the context of computing, AI and robotics. In Chapter 5, a Lefebvrian Radical Humanism is advanced by engaging in analyses of AI and robots in Post-humanism, Transhumanism, techno-deterministic approaches, social construction of technology approaches, techno-optimism, techno-pessimism, accelerationism, the mass unemployment hypothesis and Spike Jonze's movie *Her*. The chapter shows that the major lesson we can learn from the Radical Humanist sociology of technology and Henri Lefebvre's works on technology is that Radical Humanism helps creating and sustaining technologies for the many, not the few. This insight remains of high relevance in the age of digital capitalism, smart robots and AI.

Chapter 6's title is 'Policy Discourses on Robots and Artificial Intelligence (AI) in the EU, the United States, and China'. The chapter asks: How do the AI strategies of the EU, the United States under Donald Trump and China look like? It conducts a critical policy discourse analysis from a Radical Humanist Perspective. It analyses what kind of ideologies we can find in the AI strategies of the European Union, the United States under Donald Trump and China. The analysis shows that AI and robotics are situated in a digital technology race that is indicative of an international political-economic race for the accumulation of political economic power.

Chapter 7's title is 'Necropower, Death and Digital Communication in COVID-19 Capitalism'. 'The Communication of Death and Dying in Capitalist Society'. The chapter asks: What is the role of the communication of death and dying in capitalist society? How has communication with dying loved ones changed in the COVID-19 pandemic? What roles have digital technologies and capitalism played in this context?

The chapter is a reflection on the digital mediation of death and dying in the COVID-19 pandemic from a Radical

Humanist critical political economy perspective. It analyses death and dying in capitalism, discusses some foundational theoretical insights into the role of death and dying in capitalism, presents empirical studies of death and dying in society, gives a theoretical interpretation of these empirical insights, presents some empirical studies of death and dying in society and the COVID-19 pandemic and interprets their findings from a Communication Studies perspective.

In capitalist societies, death and dying are taboo topics and are hidden, invisible and institutionalised. The COVID-19 pandemic had contradictory effects on the role of death in society. It is a human, cultural and societal universal that humans want to die in company with loved ones. The presented empirical studies confirm the insights of the philosophers Kwasi Wiredu and Jürgen Habermas that humans are fundamentally social and communicative beings from the cradle to the grave. The wish to die in a social manner derives from humans' social and communicative nature. In capitalism, the reality of dying diverges from the ideal of dying. Capitalism hides, individualises, makes invisible, and institutionalises death and dying.

Building and going beyond the works of the political theorist and philosopher Achille Mbembe and the philosopher and sociologist Erich Fromm, the chapter introduces the notion of capitalist necropower. It is shown how the COVID-19 pandemic in many cases destroyed the social and communicative nature of human beings and how capitalist necropower created unnecessary surplus-deaths and formed the context of the digital mediation of communication with dying loved ones in the pandemic.

Chapter 8 is the book's conclusion. It draws together the overall arguments, argues for a radical humanism and digital humanism, and provides suggestions of how to advance these approaches in society.

2

WHAT IS HUMANISM?

1. INTRODUCTION

Contemporary society faces lots of problems that are mediated by digital technologies. These problems include, for example digital surveillance, the power and tax-avoidance strategies of transnational digital corporations, digital warfare, digital fascism, digital authoritarianism, racism and hate speech online, electronic waste and unsustainable digital economies, the exploitation of precarious digital workers, digital dictatorships, digital inequalities and divides, digital automation's precarisation of human life, attacks on quality media and the very idea of truth and news ('post-truth society', 'fake news'), etc. In a nutshell, this means that inhumanity is the central problem of contemporary digital societies. Digital Humanism promises a philosophical approach that allows us to create knowledge that supports tackling digital society's global problems.

The approach of Digital Humanism will be introduced in Chapter 3 and applied to various topics in the subsequent chapters of this book. In order to answer the question of what

Digital Humanism is, we first need to give an answer to the question: What is Humanism? This chapter discusses definitions of Humanism (Section 2). It synthesises such definitions in order to provide a philosophical understanding of Humanism. Humanism has epistemological, ontological and axiological dimensions. The chapter points out that Humanism is transcultural (Section 3). Common objections to Humanism are discussed by engaging with the works of the historian Yuval Noah Harari (Section 4). Based on the general understanding of Humanism, the approach of Radical Humanism is introduced by discussing epistemological, ontological and axiological dimensions (Section 5), and engaging with four example approaches (Section 6: Karl Marx, Erich Fromm, Wang Ruoshui, David Harvey).

2. DEFINITIONS OF HUMANISM

Let us have a look at some definitions and characterisations of Humanism from academic literature that has dealt with the question 'What is Humanism?'.

- Humanism denotes 'approaches to life – and the takers of those approaches – that were distinguished by the valuing of human beings and human culture *in contrast with* valuing gods and religion, and by affirming the effectiveness of human reason applied to evidence *in contrast with* theism, theological speculation, and revelation' (Copson 2015, 2).
- Humanism is a *system* of thought that focuses on 'the big questions' of the world and does so based on science and reason as the 'invaluable tools we can and should apply to all areas of life' (Law 2011, 6, 1).

- Humanism is an outlook on the world that stresses that 'the things which we value in human life are not an illusion; that as human beings we can find from our own resources the shared moral values which we need in order to live together, and the means to create meaningful and fulfilling lives for ourselves; and that the rejection of religious belief need not be a cause for despair' (Norman 2004, 24–25).
- Humanism is 'a philosophy or set of beliefs, that holds that human beings achieve a system of morality through their own reasoning rather than through a belief in any divine being' (Andrews 2010, 91).
- 'From the fourteenth century to the end of the nineteenth century, humanism minimally meant: (1) an educational programme founded on the classical authors and concentrating on the study of grammar, rhetoric, history, poetry and moral philosophy; (2) a commitment to the perspective, interests and centrality of human persons; (3) a belief in reason and autonomy as foundational aspects of human existence; (4) a belief that reason, scepticism and the scientific method are the only appropriate instruments for discovering truth and structuring the human community; (5) a belief that the foundations for ethics and society are to be found in autonomy and moral equality. From the end of the nineteenth century, humanism has been defined, in addition to the above, by the way in which particular aspects of core humanist belief such as human uniqueness, scientific method, reason and autonomy have been utilized in such philosophical systems as existentialism, Marxism and pragmatism' (Luik 1998).
- 'Humanism is a democratic and ethical life stance that affirms that human beings have the right and responsibility to give meaning and shape to their own lives. It stands for

the building of a more humane society through an ethics based on human and other natural values in a spirit of reason and free inquiry through human capabilities. It is not theistic, and it does not accept supernatural views of reality' (Humanists International 2020).

- 'The term "humanism" entered the philosophical vocabulary by way of the *studia humanitatis*, associated with the focus of Renaissance education on classical culture as opposed to Christian scripture. In the late nineteenth century it established itself as an umbrella term for any disposition of thought stressing the centrality of "Man" or the human species in the order of nature. Today, in the Anglophone world, humanism is more or less synonymous with atheism or secular rationalism' (Soper 2005, 167)
- Humanism 'places human beings, as opposed to God, at the center of the universe. Although a focus on human nature and human life can be traced back ultimately to ancient Greek thought, humanism in the modern sense, with its anthropocentric belief in the boundless potentiality of unfettered human reason and its secular conviction that human destiny is entirely in human hands, has its roots in the Enlightenment of the eighteenth century' (Kraye 2006, 477).

Humanism is a philosophical approach that stresses the active and transformative capacities of human beings in the social world. As philosophy, it has epistemological, ontological and axiological (ethical, moral) dimensions. Epistemology means attempts to understand how humans understand and create knowledge about the world. It is about understanding understanding. Ontology is the study of how the world looks. It is about understanding the world and being. Axiology (ethics) is moral philosophy focused on the study of the moral foundations of society, moral principles and moral practices.

Ethics is about understanding what is good and what is bad. Synthesising the characterisations of humanism cited above, we can provide the following minimum definitions of these three dimensions of Humanism as philosophy:

- *Humanism's Epistemology:*
  Humans have the capability to use reason in order to produce knowledge about how the world looks, which includes the use and development of science. Humanists critically inquire the status of the world. Critical thinking is part of the Humanist approach.
- *Humanism's Ontology:*
  Human behaviour and society are not naturally determined by God, religion, ideology or other authorities. Humans through their activities, social relations and social connections constitute society and its various forms, practices and systems.
- *Humanism's Axiology:*
  Humans have the capability and moral responsibility to create a good, humane society. Humanists are convinced that it is possible that humans act to improve society and humanity's living conditions.

3. HUMANISM'S TRANSCULTURALITY

One of the criticisms of Humanism is that it is a liberal, Eurocentric ideology. The danger of such views is that they allow us to easily dismiss the positive and important aspects of Humanism, such as the commitments to democracy, the good life and human rights for all, as Eurocentrism, which can be used for justifying authoritarianism and dictatorships. A look into history shows that Humanism has developed in many parts of the world. The claim that Humanism is Eurocentric is false.

In African thought, Humanism has played an important role. 'Long before Europeans settled in South Africa a little more than three centuries ago, indigenous African peoples had well-developed philosophical views about the worth of human beings and about desirable community relationships. A spirit of Humanism – called ubuntu (humanness) in the Zulu language and botho in the Sotho language – shaped the thoughts and daily lives of our peoples. Humanism and communal traditions together encouraged harmonious social relations' (Manogsuthu G Buthelezi, cited in: More 2004, 156).

> Botho, hunhu, ubuntu *is the central concept of social and political organization in African philosophy, particularly among the Bantu-speaking peoples. It consists of the principles of sharing and caring for one another. […] On this reasoning, we suggest that it is more correct to talk in terms of African* humanness *rather than African humanism. […] Two theses to be found in almost all indigenous African languages will be discussed here. The first is* Motho ke motho ka batho *and the second,* Feta kgomo o tshware motho. *[…] The first aphorism means that to be human is to affirm one's humanity by recognizing the humanity of others and, on that basis, establish humane respectful relations with them. Accordingly, it is* ubuntu *which constitutes the core meaning of the aphorism:* Motho ke motho ka batho. *[…] The second aphorism* (Feta kgomo o tshware motho) *means that if and when one is faced with a decisive choice between wealth and the preservation of the life of another human being, then one should opt for the preservation of life.*
>
> (Ramose 2003, 643–644)

There are also Latin American versions of Humanism. Early Latin American Humanist thinkers included Juan de Zumárraga (1468–1548) and Sor Juana Inés de la Cruz (1651–1695) (Gracia and Vargas 2018). De la Cruz challenged the religious domination of women (see Nuccetelli 2020, 29–35). Thinkers such as François-Dominique Toussaint Louverture (1743–1893) and José Martí (1854–1895) argued for anti-colonialism and anti-colonial liberation struggles and were guided by rationalism, the ideas of the Enlightenment and the French revolution (Gracia and Vargas 2018, James 1963, Nuccetelli 2020, Chapter 6). José Carlos Mariátegui (1895–1930) was a Peruvian Marxist and Socialist Humanist. He stressed the importance of class struggle and that the 'ethics of socialism is formed in the class struggle' (Mariátegui 1930; see also the essays compiled in Mariátegui 2011).

Humanism has also played an important role in Asian philosophy. In India, the ancient philosophy of Cārvāka and the Vedas advanced materialism and atheism as well as foundations of Humanism (Chatterjee and Datta 2007, chapter II; Fowler 2015, Rao 2017). In China, Humanist thought developed as part of philosophies such as Confucianism, Mohism, Taoism, Legalism, and Zen Buddhism (Fowler 2015, Guying 2018, Chapter 6; Meinert 2010, Tu 2003). Here are some examples of Chinese Humanism. Confucius was a 'moral humanist' because he grounded his ideas in 'moral psychology, action theory and virtue ethics' (Fung 2009, 270). 'The early Confucian thinkers were working toward a humanistic government that looked upon the needs of the people as its first priority' (Lai 2008, 47). 'At times, Mozi takes a more humanistic approach and appeals to the concern of heaven for all humanity. In this argument, the profile of heaven changes accordingly, from a transcendental moral authority to a loving agent that cares for the personal welfare of each human being' (Lai 2008, 65). The Confucian philosopher Mencius stressed 'humans had inherent goodness' (Lai 2008, 36).

Zen Buddhism has been interpreted as a Humanist philosophy that aims at advancing freedom from bondage and enlightenment (*satori*) (Suzuki, Fromm and De Martino 1970):

> *If we feel dissatisfied somehow with this life, if there is something in our ordinary way of living that deprives us of freedom in its most sanctified sense, we must endeavor to find a way somewhere which gives us a sense of finality and contentment. Zen proposes to do this for us and assures us of the acquirement of a new point of view in which life assumes a fresher, deeper, and more satisfying aspect. [...] satori does not consist in producing a certain pre-meditated condition by intensely thinking of it. It is the growing conscious of a new power in the mind, which enables it to judge things from a new point of view. Ever since the unfoldment of consciousness we have been led to respond to the inner and outer conditions in a certain conceptual and analytical manner. [...] Zen wants absolute freedom, even from God.*
>
> (Suzuki 2015, 15, 34, 36)

In classical European philosophy, Aristotle was the most important representative of Humanism (Freeman 2015). In the Islamic World of the Middle Ages, Humanism developed as part of the thought of, for example the Mu'tazila, Abu Nasr Al-Farabi, Ibn Miskawayh, Ibn Sina (Avicenna), Ibn Rushd (Averroes) (Ljamai 2015).

As this shows, Humanism has not only been Western and liberal; there are different versions of it, including a variety of Humanisms that originated in Africa, Latin America and Asia. Humanism is not necessarily a liberal worldview, there are a variety of worldviews underpinning it, which has besides Liberal Humanism resulted in, for example Religious Humanisms, Socialist Humanism and Marxist Humanism. Luik (1998) lists four types of modern Humanist philosophy: Marxist Humanism, Pragmatic Humanism, Existentialist Humanism and Heideggerian Humanism. 'Among the great humanists of the past were Buddha, the Hebrew Prophets, Jesus Christ, Socrates, the philosophers of the Renaissance, and those of the Enlightenment down to Goethe and Marx. There is an unbroken tradition of humanism which reaches back some 2500 years and which is now growing in the most divergent fields of thought' (Fromm 1961/2003, 204). Humanism has many entry points that should all be acknowledged ideationally and institutionally. Humanism should best be organised as transdisciplinary and transcultural encounter, debate and co-operation projects.

There continue to be major critiques of Humanism.

4. YUVAL NOAH HARARI'S CRITIQUE OF HUMANISM

Slavoj Žižek (2016, 22) identifies four types of and stages in the development of anti-Humanism:

1. theocentric anti-Humanism: religious fundamentalisms that oppose secularism;
2. theoretical anti-Humanism: French structuralism and post-structuralism, whose main representatives were Althusser, Foucault and Lacan;
3. deep-ecological anti-Humanism: environmental movements that reduce humans 'to just one of the animal species' and blames humanity as such for having 'derailed the balance of life on Earth' (Žižek 2016, 22);

4. Post-humanism and Transhumanism: '"Posthumanists" (Donna Haraway and others) are cultural theorists who note how today's social and technological progress more and more undermines our human exclusivity [...] So while, for posthumanists, "humans" are a weird species of animal cyborgs, "transhumanists" (Ray Kurzweil and others) refer to recent scientific and technological innovations (AI, digitalization) which point towards the emergence of a Singularity, a new type of collective intelligence' (Žižek 2016, 22).

The historian Yuval Noah Harari (2017, 2011) is a representative of the fourth form of anti-Humanism. He writes popular bestsellers about the history and future of humanity. He challenges Humanism (Harari 2011, Chapter 12; Harari 2017, Chapter 7) and advances a version of Post-humanism that sees the end of humanity and humans and their replacement by cyborgs and Dataism as inevitable consequences of scientific progress. He argues that there will be the 'upgrading of humans into gods' (Harari 2017, 50) that are immortal. 'In the twenty-first century, the third big project of humankind will be to acquire for us divine powers of creation and destruction, and upgrade *Homo sapiens* into *Homo deus*' (53). 'Yet once authority shifts from humans to algorithms, the humanist projects may become irrelevant. Once we abandon the homo-centric world view in favour of a data-centric world view, human health and happiness may seem far less important. [...] Dataism thereby threatens to do to *Homo sapiens* what *Homo sapiens* has done to all other animals' (459–460). Harari characterises Humanism as a religion that 'worships humanity' (259). He identifies three forms of humanism: Liberal Humanism that resulted in capitalism and individualism, Socialist Humanism that resulted in Stalin's gulags and Evolutionary Humanism that brought about Social

Darwinism, Hitler and Auschwitz. Harari speaks of 'the three humanist sects' (306).

Harari advances a cynical form of reason that seems to assume that Humanism is the source of all evils in the world. He argues that as the consequence of an unstoppable, science-based negative dialectic of Humanism, the human being and, along with it, Humanism will soon disappear, and humans can do nothing about it. The socialist writer Paul Mason (2019, 143) characterises Harari's approach as a 'fatalism' that 'will, if unchallenged, leave us disarmed against the ongoing power grabs of tech monopolies and surveillance states'.

Harari mischaracterises Humanism. Stalin and Hitler were not Humanists. Many Stalinists have opposed both Humanism and Socialist Humanism. And Socialist Humanists have opposed both Stalinism and fascism and have been ardent supporters of democracy. In a detailed socio-psychological study, Erich Fromm shows that Hitler was a necrophile and that the 'necrophile demands *annihilation*' (Fromm 1973/1997, 406), that Stalin was a mental and physical sadist, and that both stand for human destructiveness, a characteristic for authoritarianism that is opposed to Humanism. Harari sets up Humanism as a straw man by including the major modern worldviews and political projects in it. Such a broad characterisation, however, deprives the notion of Humanism of its meaningfulness.

Humanism has the potential to take on new forms that help us to challenge new fascisms and the totalitarian potentials of Dataism. Based on the elaborated understanding of Humanism, the next section introduces Radical Humanism. We will approach the question of Radical Humanism by first engaging with its foundations (Section 5) and second by having a look at four specific Radical Humanist approaches (Section 6: Karl Marx, Erich Fromm, Wang Ruoshui, David Harvey).

5. WHAT IS RADICAL HUMANISM? FOUNDATIONS OF RADICAL HUMANISM

The main points of criticism of Humanism are that it is (1) at the epistemological level advancing positivism, is (2) at the ontological level advancing, idealising and ideologically justifying individualism, capitalism and egoism, and is (3) at the axiological level advancing a particularistic form of universalism that restricts the question of what it means to be human to white, male, Western bourgeois individuals and a concept of nature as wild and domesticable, which has advanced racism, sexism, patriarchy, (neo-)colonialism, imperialism, capitalism, classism and environmental destruction. This critique was not, as many mistakenly assume, first formulated by Post-Structuralists, Post-Colonialism and Post-Humanism. Already in the nineteenth century, Karl Marx criticised Liberal Humanism.

Enlightenment Humanism is a philosophical approach that is based on the insight that the development of society and humans is not predetermined by God's will but that human reason is the decisive criterion that shapes the development of society and humans. Enlightenment philosophers included, for example Jean le Rond d'Alembert, George Berkeley, Marquis de Condorcet, Étienne Bonnot de Condillac, René Descartes, Denis Diderot, Johann Wolfgang von Goethe, Johann Gottfried Herder, Wilhelm von Humboldt, David Hume, Thomas Jefferson, Immanuel Kant, Gottfried Wilhelm Leibniz, John Locke, Montesquieu, Thomas Paine, Jean-Jacques Rousseau, Adam Smith or Voltaire.[1] They argued that the 'central concern of human existence was not the discovery of God's will, but the shaping of human life and society according to reason' (Luik 1998). 'Enlightenment humanism comes closest

1 https://en.wikipedia.org/wiki/Category:Enlightenment_philosophers.

to agreement in its ethical and political maxims in its commitment to the discipline of reason in which truth must emerge, both publicly and privately, not through dogma but through argument and counter-argument, and in its commitment to the virtues of beneficence and non-malfeasance' (Luik 1998). Enlightenment Humanism was the worldview that shaped the rise of representative democracy as alternative to monarchical and clerical rule and the rise of capitalism as alternative to feudalism.

Marx criticises that Liberal Humanism, understood as the liberalism of property – i.e. the right that everyone can possess as much property, wealth and capital as they please – results in possessive individualism, an egoism that harms the public good.

> Liberty in bourgeois society '*is the liberty of man viewed as an isolated monad, withdrawn into himself. […] The practical application of the right of liberty is the right of* private property'.
>
> (Marx 1843, 162–163)

> *The right of man to private property is, therefore, the right to enjoy one's property and to dispose of it at one's discretion* (à son gré), *without regard to other men, independently of society, the right of self-interest.*
>
> (Marx 1843, 163)

> *The sphere of circulation or commodity exchange, within whose boundaries the sale and purchase of labour-power goes on, is in fact a very Eden of the innate rights of man. It is the exclusive realm of Freedom, Equality, Property and Bentham. Freedom, because both buyer and seller of a commodity, let us*

say of labour-power, are determined only by their own free will. They contract as free persons, who are equal before the law. Their contract is the final result in which their joint will finds a common legal expression. Equality, because each enters into relation with the other, as with a simple owner of commodities, and they exchange equivalent for equivalent. Property, because each disposes only of what is his own. And Bentham, because each looks only to his own advantage. The only force bringing them together, and putting them into relation with each other, is the selfishness, the gain and the private interest of each. Each pays heed to himself only, and no one worries about the others.

(Marx 1867, 280)

Marx also argues that capitalism is based on the looting of colonies and slavery: 'The treasures captured outside Europe by undisguised looting, enslavement and murder flowed back to the mother-country and were turned into capital there' (Marx 1867, 918). The bourgeois political economist and capitalists would tolerate the poverty of the colonised and slavery, which would unmask the proclaimed Humanism of Liberalism as inhumanity: 'In the interest of the so-called wealth of the nation, he seeks for artificial means to ensure the poverty of the people. Here his apologetic armour crumbles off, piece by piece, like rotten touchwood' (Marx 1867, 932).

Marx also stressed that capitalism results in the destruction of nature: 'Capitalist production, therefore, only develops the techniques and the degree of combination of the social process of production by simultaneously undermining the original sources of all wealth – the soil and the worker' (Marx 1867, 638). Capitalist production requires labour-power and physical resources. Capitalists are compelled to try to obtain both as cheaply as possible in order to survive on the market and accumulate, which results in the development of ever newer methods of exploiting labour, and appropriating nature cheaply or for free.

Liberalism declares private property as 'one of the rights of man' (Marx and Engels 1845/1846, 208). Given capital's effects, private property and capital only have 'a liberal appearance' (Marx and Engels 1845/1846, 208), but in reality are barbaric.

Based on Marx, the critical theorists Max Horkheimer and Theodor W. Adorno (2002) analysed the negative dialectic of Liberal Humanism. They speak of the dialectic of Enlightenment, by which they mean that capitalism's political economy creates destructive potentials and realities that destroy and undermine the realisation of human rights that the Enlightenment and liberalism promise. Capitalism entails the tendency of the 'self-destruction of enlightenment' (Horkheimer and Adorno 2002, xvi) so that there is the potential for 'the reversion of enlightened civilization to barbarism' (xix). Coldness is 'the basic principle of bourgeois subjectivity, without which there could have been no Auschwitz' (Adorno 1973/2004, 363).

Capitalism's structures of exploitation and domination turn against Liberalism's Enlightenment values and, in the twentieth century, resulted in Auschwitz. 'After the brief interlude of liberalism in which the bourgeois kept one another in check, power is revealing itself as archaic terror in a fascistically rationalized form' (Horkheimer and Adorno 2002, 68). Horkheimer and Adorno point out that capitalist society believes in and promises liberty, equality and fraternity, yet the capitalist reality are possessive individualism and inequalities – an antagonism between the freedom of property on the one hand and social freedom, equality and solidarity on the other hand. The result is that fascist potentials can germinate within capitalism.

The alternative to Liberal Humanism is not – as many Postmodernists proclaim – that we should bury the ideas of modernity, universalism, truth, solidarity, Humanism, the Western world and emancipation. Doing so easily results in an anti-modernism that idealises toil, particularism and relativism that contribute to a fragmenting society and deepening divides, reactionary attacks on knowledge-producing institutions in education, the media and culture that have parallels with the far-right, and the support of dictatorships in the name of the opposition to Euro- and Western-centrism and anti-imperialism.

The alternative is an alternative modernity, a fully universal Humanism, and global emancipation from exploitation and domination that benefits all. Radical Humanism is the proper alternative to liberal humanism. But what is Radical Humanism?

Radical Humanism is a materialist philosophy that stresses the productive, social and transformative capacities of human beings that enable them to liberate themselves from class society, capitalism, exploitation, domination and ideology and to together create a better world. Socialist Humanism is another term used for Radical Humanism. It has three dimensions (see Alderson and Spencer 2017, Fromm 1965b, Fuchs 2020a):

- *Radical Humanism's Epistemology: Dialectical Epistemology*
  Radical Humanism uses dialectical philosophy, critique of the political economy and ideology critique as intellectual means for critically understanding society and the world. It is interested in the development of critical theories of society and the critical analysis of exploitation and domination.

Humans have the capability to use reason in order to produce knowledge about how the world looks, which includes the use and development of science. Humanists critically inquire the status of the world. Critical thinking is part of the Humanist approach.

- *Radical Humanism's Ontology: The Human as Social, Societal, Producing Being*
  Radical Humanism conceives of the human being as a social and societal being and of society as the realm of human social production. Society is made by humans in social relations, which means that it changes and that humans have the capacity to change society actively through co-operation and if needed through social struggles. Radical Humanism stresses the roles of human interests, human needs, human practices, praxis and social production in society. Many Radical Humanists have found inspiration in Marx's (1844b) *Economic and Philosophic Manuscripts.* The human being is not conceived as an isolated monad, but as a social being existing in and through social relations. Also humans making society is interpreted as meaning that humans 'make their own history, but they do not make it as they please; they do not make it under circumstances chosen by themselves, but under circumstances directly encountered, given and transmitted from the past' (Marx 1852, 103).

  The Radical Humanist analysis of class and dominative societies utilises the notion of alienation. Alienation means that workers are not in control of the means of production (class society), citizens are not in control of collective decision-making (dictatorship) and humans are not in control of meaning-making and definition-power (ideology, disrespect). The results are exploitation and domination. The exploitation of humans in class relations is the key to understanding the economic form of alienation. But alienation also takes on the form of domination in the political system, where one group oppresses other groups, and the form of ideology in the cultural system. These forms of alienation interact. Capitalism, patriarchy and racism are three types of power relations that each combine economic alienation, political alienation and cultural alienation. In contemporary society, capitalism, patriarchy and racism interact in capitalist society. In societies shaped by class and alienation, humans are exploited and oppressed by the ruling class.

- *Radical Humanism's Axiology: The Philosophy of Praxis*
The philosophy of praxis is Radical Humanism's axiology. It stresses that besides all their differences, human beings have a great deal in common, including the desire and need for happiness and leading a good life, which given the human being's social nature implies that everyone should be able to lead a good life. Humans can only achieve a better society through making their own history in the form of class struggles for a classless society. Praxis is class struggle for democratic socialism. Radical Humanism is a Humanism that stresses the need to create conditions in society that allow all humans and society to flourish and fully realise their potentials. Humanism is socialism. Socialism is Humanism. Socialism denotes a society of the commons, where all humans benefit. Socialism is a realisation of the economic, political and cultural commons. In a socialist society, all humans live in wealth and toil is reduced, minimised and abolished (economic commons). In such a society, all humans have democratic participation rights (political commons) and are respected (cultural commons). Democratic socialism sees socialism as inherently Humanist and democratic. It is anti-fascist, anti-Stalinist and opposed

to possessive individualism. It is critical of anti-democratic potentials and realities. Radical Humanism doesn't limit the understanding of democracy to the political system, but argues for the extension of democracy to society at large, including the economy. Radical Humanism stresses the democratic need for the collective self-management of the economy and society. It understands democracy as participatory democracy. Radical Humanism's ethics is an ethics of class and social struggles. Convinced that humans deserve and need a society that benefits all, it argues that it is worth and necessary that humans struggle for democratic socialism.

6. FOUR APPROACHES TO RADICAL HUMANISM: KARL MARX, ERICH FROMM, WANG RUOSHUI, DAVID HARVEY

Let us have a closer look at Radical Humanism through the works of Karl Marx, Erich Fromm and Wang Ruoshui. Marx (1818–1883) was 'a humanist through and through' (Fromm 1961/2003, 68) and the thinker who most influenced Radical Humanism. Erich Fromm (1900–1980) was a critical theorist and Humanist philosopher who was influenced by the works of Marx and Sigmund Freud. He did a lot for advancing Radical Humanism. For example, he edited the collected volume *Socialist Humanism: An International Symposium* (Fromm 1965b) and in contrast to structural Marxists such as Louis Althusser pointed out the Humanist aspects of Marx's thoughts (Fromm 1961/2003). Wang Ruoshui (1926–2002) was a Chinese philosopher, who was one of the main representatives of Marxist Humanism in China. In the early 1980s, he was involved in an intellectual debate on Humanism and alienation. David Harvey (born in 1935) is a political economist, social theorist and economic geographer. He is one of the most cited and most influential social scientists. His work is focused on the analysis of capitalism.

6.1 Karl Marx

Marx argues that in class societies, humans are incompletely social and the full potentials of humans and society cannot be realised. Socialism is 'fully developed humanism' (Marx 1844b, 296) and abolishes the *dehumanised* being (284). It requires the 'annihilation of the *estranged* character' (341) of society and 'the *positive* transcendence of *private property* as *human self-estrangement*' (296). The commitment to praxis, i.e. class and social struggle, is Socialist Humanism's categorical imperative:

> *To be radical is to grasp the root of the matter. But for man the root is man himself. [...] The criticism of religion ends with the teaching that* man is the highest being for man, *hence with the* categorical imperative to overthrow all relations *in which man is a debased, enslaved, forsaken, despicable being, relations which cannot be better described than by the exclamation of a Frenchman when it was planned to introduce a tax on dogs: Poor dogs! They want to treat you like human beings!*
>
> (Marx 1844a, 182)

> *Where, then, is the* positive *possibility of [...] emancipation?*
>
> Answer: *In the formation of a class with* radical chains, *a class of civil society which is not a class of*

> *civil society, an estate which is the dissolution of all estates, a sphere which has a universal character by its universal suffering and claims no* particular right *because no* particular wrong *but* wrong generally *is perpetrated against it; [...] a sphere, finally, which cannot emancipate itself without emancipating itself from all other spheres of society and thereby emancipating all other spheres of society, which, in a word, is the* complete loss *of man and hence can win itself only through the* complete rewinning of man. *This dissolution of society as a particular estate is the* proletariat.
>
> (Marx 1844a, 186)

6.2 Erich Fromm

Fromm (1947/2003) distinguishes between Humanistic ethics and authoritarian ethics. Authoritarians are convinced of the principled that 'an authority states what is good for man and lays down the laws and norms of conduct', while for Humanists the human being is 'both the norm giver and the subject of the norms' (Fromm 1947/2003, 6). Humanist ethics 'is based on the principle that "good" is what is good for man and "evil" what is detrimental to man; the *sole* criterion *of ethical* value being man's welfare' (13).

Fromm (1976/1997) characterises a Humanist Socialist society as the transition from societies of having to societies of being. He outlines some constituents of such a society:

> *...the goal is not control over nature but control over technique and over irrational social forces and institutions that threaten the survival of Western*

society, if not of the human race. […] production shall be directed for the sake of 'sane consumption'. […] Sane consumption is possible only if we can drastically curb the right of the stockholders and management of big enterprises to determine their production solely on the basis of profit and expansion. […] To achieve a society based on being, all people must actively participate in their economic function and as citizens. Hence, our liberation from the having mode of existence is possible only through the full realization of industrial and political participatory democracy. […] Active and responsible participation further requires that humanistic management replace bureaucratic management. […] All brainwashing methods in industrial and political advertising must be prohibited. […] we must prohibit the use of all hypnoid forms of propaganda, for commodities as well as for politicians. […] The gap between the rich and the poor nations must be closed. […] Many of the evils of present-day capitalist and communist societies would disappear with the introduction of a guaranteed yearly income. […] Women must be liberated from patriarchal domination. […] A Supreme Cultural Council, charged with the task of advising the government, the politicians, and the citizens in all matters in which knowledge is necessary, should be established. […] A system of effective dissemination of effective information must also be established. […] Scientific research must be separated from application in industry and defense. […] atomic disarmament.
(Fromm 1997, 142–143, 145, 147, 150, 152, 153, 154, 155, 157, 159)

6.3 Wang Ruoshui

Wang Ruoshui (1984a, 1984b) stresses the importance of the concept of alienation in Marxist Humanism and the importance of Marx's *Economic and Philosophic Manuscripts*. Humans create something that becomes a 'dissident force, going beyond the people's control' (Wang 1984b, 30). Exploitation and class relations constitute economic alienation, which is the most fundamental form of alienation (29). Wang points out that for Marx, there are also political alienation (e.g. bureaucratic state power that becomes the master of the people and serves special interests instead of the public interest) and ideological alienation (e.g. personality cult). The three forms of alienation are not automatically abolished by the abolition of capitalism, alienation can persist (29). In 'a socialist society there exists the possibility of the emergence of alienation not only in ideology and politics but even in the economic field' (34). Wang (1984a) argues that for Marx, the human being is the starting point, but not as abstract being, but as 'real and practical' being 'living under certain social relations' (40). Wang argues that this focus on the human being shaped Marx's entire approach in that it criticises how the human being and its interests are subordinated under capital and private property in capitalist society and bourgeois political economy. Practically speaking, this means that the capitalist is only interested in the exploitation of human labour-power not the human being as such. In Socialist Humanism, the human being 'is not the means but the end' (Wang 1984a, 42). The global problems are also the outcome of alienation processes: 'Exploitation constitutes alienation, but it is only one form of alienation; there are also other forms of alienation. None of today's global issues – such as environmental pollution, the population explosion, nuclear weapons and the North-South confrontation – are natural disasters. Instead, they are scourges created by mankind itself, and are the results of the alienation of human behaviour' (Wang 1997, 88).

6.4 David Harvey

Wang Ruoshoi stresses the importance of Marx's concept of alienation for a critique of society. More recently, David Harvey has argued that alienation is a universal feature of contemporary capitalism that shapes not just economic production relations but also consumption, surplus-value realisation, the distribution and consumption of commodities, finance, frustrations with politics, unaffordable public services, nationalist ideology, racism, police violence, militarism, warfare, alcoholism, suicide, depression, bureaucracy, pollution, gentrification, climate change etc. 'Alienation is everywhere. It exists at work in production, at home in consumption, and it dominates much of politics and daily life' (Harvey 2018, 429). The major danger of universal alienation is that it advances fascist potentials. 'With mass alienation, somebody like Trump could come along and blast his way into power. [...] Trump is the President of alienation' (Harvey 2018, 429).

All of the problems of universal alienation are based on and linked to capitalism but cannot be reduced to it. Marx was critical of ethics and morality because they often operate as ideology that keeps humans from social struggles. But his categorical imperative is a Radical Humanist principle of morality: act and engage in social struggles in order to overcome alienation in society. Marx's ethics is an ethics of social struggle, the philosophy of praxis. The goal of praxis is democratic socialism. The longer passage from Erich Fromm cited above outlines the contours of democratic socialism.

Democratic socialism is not a dictatorship but a participatory democracy where alienation is abolished and humans and technologies are put to use for the benefit of all, and humans collectively manage political economy.

David Harvey (2014) advances a radical Marxist-humanist perspective. In contrast to structuralist and functionalist approaches that primarily stress that crises are collapse and breakdown tendencies of capitalism, Harvey emphasises praxis, i.e. the importance of class and social struggles for advancing equality. Harvey stresses that 'class struggle' is 'central to the politics of radical egalitarianism' (Harvey 2010, 234). 'The accumulation of capital will never cease. it will have to be stopped. [...] To do what has to be done will take tenacity and determination, patience and cunning, along with fierce political commitments born out of moral outrage at what exploitative compound growth is doing to all facets of life, human and otherwise, on planet earth. Political mobilisations sufficient to such a task have occurred in the past. They can and will surely come again' (Harvey 2010, 260). Harvey argues that what is needed for advancing Humanism is 'an anti-neoliberal movement' (Harvey 2014, 266), a 'piecemeal approach' that advances 'ecologically sensitive relations', 'far higher levels of social justice and democratic governance' (Harvey 2014, 266). Such a movement

> *...proposes a peaceful and non-violent move towards social change of the sort initially witnessed in the early stages of Tahrir, Syntagma and Taksim Squares [...] It seeks to bring people together strategically around common but limited themes. [...] imagine what the world would be like if the domination of exchange value and the alienated behaviours that attach to the pursuit of money power as Keynes described them were simultaneously reduced and the*

> *powers of private persons to profit from social wealth were radically curbed. imagine, further, if the alienations of the contemporary work experience, of a compensatory consumption that can never satisfy, of untold levels of economic inequality and discordance in the relation to nature, were all diminished by a rising wave of popular discontent with capital's current excesses. We would then be living in a more humane world with much-reduced levels of social inequality and conflict and much-diminished political corruption and oppression.*
> (Harvey 2014, 266)

Harvey argues for a Radical Humanism. 'The belief that we can through conscious thought and action change both the world we live in and ourselves for the better defines a humanist tradition. [...] Humanism, both religious and secular, is a world view that measures its achievements in terms of the liberation of human potentialities, capacities and powers' (Harvey 2014, 282–283).

Harvey is aware of and critical of the ideological abuses of the concept of the human that has turned into inhumanity by denying certain human groups equality so that 'some deluded beings believe that we, being next to God, are *Übermenschen* having dominion over the universe. This form of humanism becomes even more pernicious when identifiable groups in a population are not considered worthy of being considered human. This was the fate of many indigenous populations in the Americas as they faced colonial settlers. Designated as "savages", they were considered a part of nature and not a part of humanity' (Harvey 2014, 283).

But other than quite some Post-humanists, Post-modernists and Post-structuralists, Harvey does not conclude that one should abolish Humanism, but rather argues that such approaches are no Humanism at all and that we need to radicalise Humanism and struggle for realising the dialectics of universalism and particularities:

> *No social order can, therefore, evade the question of universals. The contemporary 'radical' critique of universalism is sadly misplaced. It should focus instead on the specific institutions of power that translate between particularity and universality rather than attack universalism per se.*
>
> (Harvey 2000, 242)

> *Dialectics here is useful. It teaches that universality always exists* in relation to *particularity: neither can be separated from the other even though they are distinctive moments within our conceptual operations and practical engagements.*
>
> (Harvey 2000, 241)

Radical Humanism implies the struggle for a humane, just, social and fair society: 'Oligarchic capitalist class privilege and power are taking the world in a similar direction almost everywhere. Political power backed by intensifying surveillance, policing and militarised violence is being used to attack the well-being of whole populations deemed expendable and disposable. We are daily witnessing the systematic dehumanisation of disposable people. [...] There are, as we have seen, enough compelling contradictions within capital's domain to foster many grounds for hope' (Harvey 2014, 292, 293).

A Radical Humanist society includes, among other organisational features, the following ones:

- 'common rights regimes – with particular emphasis upon human knowledge and the land as the most crucial commons we have – the creation, management and protection of which lie in the hands of popular assemblies and associations' (Harvey 2014, 295);

- 'Daily life is slowed down – locomotion shall be leisurely and slow – to maximise time for free activities conducted in a stable and well-maintained environment protected from dramatic episodes of creative destruction' (Harvey 2014, 295);
- 'New technologies and organisational forms are created that lighten the load of all forms of social labour, dissolve unnecessary distinctions in technical divisions of labour, liberate time for free individual and collective activities, and diminish the ecological footprint of human activities' (Harvey 2014, 295).
- 'Everyone should have equal entitlements to education, health care, housing, food security, basic goods and open access to transportation to ensure the material basis for freedom from want and for freedom of action and movement' (Harvey 2014, 296):

7. CONCLUSION

This chapter asked: What is Humanism? For giving an answer, minimum definitions of Humanism were established that have three dimensions (epistemology, ontology, axiology). Humanism is a philosophical approach that stresses the active and transformative capacities of human beings in the social world.

This chapter argued for Radical Humanism. Radical/Socialist Humanism is a materialist philosophy that stresses the productive, social and transformative capacities of human beings that enable them to liberate themselves from class society, capitalism, exploitation, domination and ideology and to together create a better world.

Given the global problems societies and humanity face today, we urgently need to ask moral questions: What is a good society? What needs to be done so that we establish a good society? What have been the major factors that have prevented the establishment of a good society? What should we do in order to advance a good society? Radical Humanism is a philosophical approach that helps us to reflect on these questions. In the age of inhumanity, we need to renew Humanism.

3

WHAT IS DIGITAL HUMANISM?

1. INTRODUCTION

Chapter 2 asked: What is Humanism? It pointed out that in order to solve the global problems, we need a Radical Humanism. While traditional liberal and individualistic Humanism is based on a negative dialectic that calls forth global inequalities as well as destructive and fascist potentials, Radical Humanism poses an alternative that aims at creating a society where all benefit.

Contemporary society faces lots of problems that are mediated by digital technologies. These problems include, for example digital surveillance, the power and tax-avoidance strategies of transnational digital corporations, digital warfare, digital fascism, digital authoritarianism, racism and hate speech online, electronic waste and unsustainable digital economies, the exploitation of precarious digital workers, digital dictatorships, digital inequalities and divides, digital automation's precarisation of human life, attacks on quality media and the very idea of truth and news ('post-truth society', 'fake news'), etc. In a nutshell, this means that inhumanity is the central problem of contemporary digital societies. Digital

Humanism promises a philosophical approach that allows us to create knowledge that supports tackling digital society's global problems.

This chapter deals with the question: What is Digital Humanism? It argues that Digital Humanism is a philosophy suited for the analysis of the digital age that has specific epistemological, ontological and axiological dimensions. It also introduces a specific version of Digital Humanism, namely Radical Digital Humanism. It argues that we need to advance the co-operation of all Humanisms in order to circumvent the rise of new fascisms in the digital age. Section 2 asks: What is Digital Humanism? Section 3 asks: What is Radical Digital Humanism? Section 4 asks: What objections are there to Digital Humanism? Section 5 draws some conclusions.

The next section deals with the question: What is Digital Humanism?

2. FOUNDATIONS OF DIGITAL HUMANISM: WHAT IS DIGITAL HUMANISM?

Digital domination and digital capitalism threaten humanity. There is the exploitation of digital labour; the violation of privacy and the commodification of big data as capital accumulation of the digital giants, the world's largest digital corporations; the circulation of digital fascism on social media; the AI-based automation of labour that has the potential to increase human misery; corporate and political digital surveillance; digital warfare; the massive production of electronic waste and the powering of digital technologies by fossil fuel–based forms of energy and nuclear energy, which exacerbates the environmental crisis; etc. As a consequence, the survival of humanity and its natural and social environments are endangered.

Humanism is a force that is today much needed in order to oppose the dangers humanity faces. Thus far, there has only been little use of the notion of 'Digital Humanism' for opposing digital destruction, digital domination, digital exploitation and digital authoritarianism. This chapter is the attempt to contribute to the popularisation of the notion of Digital Humanism in academic and public discourse.

In August 2021, a title search for 'Digital Humanism' in Web of Science resulted in five results.[1] Three of them (Mayer 2019, Plaul 2019, Widdau 2019) are reviews of the book *Digitaler Humanismus. Eine Ethik für das Zeitalter der Künstlichen Intelligenz (Digital Humanism. Ethics for the Age of Artificial Intelligence,* Nida-Rümelin and Weidenfeld 2018). The two other publications are comments on how to think about Digital Humanism (Porter 2018, Rodríguez-Ortega 2018).

Rodríguez-Ortega's (2018) paper is the introduction to the proceedings of a Digital Humanities conference. It interprets the Digital Humanities as 'a new digital humanism project' (1). The basic argument is that the Digital Humanities combine 'critical thinking and action' (2) with the application of databases, digitised collections and archives, algorithms, neural networks, big data analytics and software. The basic problem of big data analytics, the Digital Humanities and Computational Social Science is their technological fetishism that often does not leave enough time and space for the

1 Data source: title search for 'Digital Humanism' in Web of Science, https://www.webofscience.com, accessed on 5 August 2021. A simultaneous search in Google Scholar resulted in some more results, but confirmed the overall insight that until August 2021, little had been published under the title of 'digital humanism'.

development of critical theories of the digital, which results in a new positivism – digital positivism (Fuchs 2017). The danger of these approaches is that they are so much focused on computational and quantitative methods that Humanism is reduced to positivism and scientism and forgets critical theory and the critique of quantification's role in capitalism and administration. Rodríguez-Ortega (2018, p. 3) argues that the Digital Humanities also mean the co-operation of 'humans and non-humans (algorithms, neural networks, programming languages, coding systems)'. Such an understanding leaves Humanism and is a Post-humanist, Actor Network Theory-based devaluation of humans that compares them to machines. Digital machines do not have consciousness, morality and critical thinking. The danger of Digital Humanities and Computational Social Science is the destruction of the foundations of Humanism. Similar to Rodríguez-Ortega, Porter understands Digital Humanism as Digital Humanities. He focuses on the implications for psychology and argues that digital technologies 'offer rich materials for humanistic interpretation, and they can never supplant it' (Porter 2018, 372).

Julian Nida-Rümelin is a philosopher, Nathalie Weidenfeld a film scholar. In their co-authored book on Digital Humanism (Rümelin and Weidenfeld 2018), the two authors combine their two fields so that foundations of a practical Humanist ethics of Artificial Intelligence (AI) are presented and illustrated by examples from science fiction movies. The book analyses how robots and AI are said to change society, what potentials these technologies actually do and do not have and how they should and should not be used. Robot ethics and AI ethics are subfields of digital ethics, which means that the book by Nida-Rümelin and Weidenfeld covers one aspect of Digital Humanism. The basic ethical principle the book is based on is the following one: 'Digital Humanism does not transform humans into machines and does not interpret machines as humans. It holds on to the specificity of the human being and its abilities and uses digital technologies to expand them, not to defeat them. […] The human form of existence is not an annex to technical development, rather it is the great challenge of our responsibility to shape digitalisation in such a way that it contributes to the humanisation of the world'[2] (Rümelin and Weidenfeld 2018, 11).

The Digital Humanism Initiative emerged at Vienna University of Technology and was initiated by Hannes Werthner, who is professor emeritus of e-commerce and former Dean of the Faculty of Informatics. This initiative resulted in the Vienna Manifesto on Digital Humanism that says:

> *The time is right to bring together humanistic ideals with critical thoughts about technological progress. We therefore link this manifesto to the intellectual tradition of humanism and similar movements striving for an enlightened humanity. […] We must shape technologies in accordance with human values and needs, instead of allowing technologies to shape humans. Our task is not only to rein in the downsides of information and communication technologies, but to encourage human-centered innovation. We call for a Digital Humanism that describes, analyzes, and, most importantly, influences*

2 Translation from German: „Ein digitaler Humanismus transformiert den Menschen nicht in eien Maschine und interpretiert Maschinen nicht als Menschen. Er hält an der Besonderheit des Menschen und seiner Fähigkeiten fest und bedient sich der digitalen Technologien, um diese zu erweitern, nicht um diese zu bescrhänken. […] Die menschliche Existenzform ist nicht Annex technischer Entwicklung, vielmehr ist es die große Herausforderung unserer Verantwortlichkeit, die Digitalisierung so zu gestalten, dass sie zur Humanisierung der Welt beiträgt".

> *the complex interplay of technology and humankind, for a better society and life, fully respecting universal human rights.*
>
> (Digital Humanism Initiative 2019)

Publications, a manifesto, events, public debates and, above all, ever more inhumane developments in digital society show that there is a certain desire and need for renewing Humanism in the digital age. Digital Humanism is a philosophical approach that stresses the active and transformative capacities of human beings in the digital age. Based on the characterisation of Humanism as philosophy in the previous chapter, we can now characterise the three dimensions of Digital Humanism:

- *Digital Humanism's Epistemology:*
  Computer technologies and machines in general are different from humans. They do not have reason, consciousness, morality and critical thinking. Artificial Intelligence, robots, big data, computational and digital methods can and should not replace the importance of the human being in society. They cannot, like humans, critically inquire the status of the world.
- *Digital Humanism's Ontology:*
  Technologies in general and computers in particular are not human, social and societal beings. Human beings and their activities, social relations and connections constitute society. In contemporary societies digital technologies shape and are shaped by humans and their social relations, but such technologies are not autonomous actors and are different from humans, which is why digital machines should not be analysed as if they were humans and humans should not be analysed as if they were machines. In

techno-social systems, humans and machines interact based on human practices that create this system.

- *Digital Humanism's Axiology:*
  Given that digital machines are not humans and humans are not machines, it is a moral imperative *not to treat* machines as humans and not to treat humans as machines. Contemporary society's problems partly have to do with such reductions. Digital machines are not the causes and not the solution to society's problems. Society and digital society should be organised in manners that allow the establishment of a good, humane society. Digital technologies should be shaped and used in manners that do not harm society and humans, but rather support the establishment of a good, humane society.

The philosopher of information Wolfgang Hofkirchner (2021) argues that in the debate on AI and technology in general, there are conflationist, disconnectivist and dialectical positions. Conflationists claim there are no differences between technologies and humans. Disconnectivists argue for a dualism of technologies and humans. They say that technologies and humans constitute two separate realms of existence. Dialectical positions argue that 'techno-social systems integrate humans and machines' (43). Hofkirchner points out that both humans and machines are physical and processual systems, but that humans show agency, whereas machines do not. Humans make choices and are 'social agents' (44) who actively transform society. He argues for an alter-humanism that is 'affirming both the identity of, and the difference between, the two sides, humans and machines, as done by combinations. Combinations provide the proper basis for a humanism that is up to the challenges of digitalisation – Digital Humanism' (45–46).

Most Digital Humanists will be able to subscribe to the suggested general tasks of Digital Humanism, so what I suggest is a minimum consensus of Digital Humanists and a minimum core definition of Digital Humanism. Digital Humanism is still a relatively new approach to digital ethics, which means that in the future a variety of approaches to Digital Humanism will emerge that are influenced by different worldviews, philosophies and cultures. I suggest that the three dimensions of Digital Humanism can be the joint starting point for the dialogue between and co-operation of different versions of Digital Humanism. Most importantly, they all share the opposition to inhumanities in the digital age. Transdisciplinary and transcultural co-operation in Digital Humanism is needed in order to circumvent the dangers of a new fascism, the escalation of the global problems and the destruction of society and humanity.

The next section engages with the question: What is Radical Digital Humanism?

3. FOUNDATIONS OF RADICAL DIGITAL HUMANISM

Taking the work of Radical Humanists such as Karl Marx, Erich Fromm and David Harvey as the starting point, the present author's approach to Digital Humanism is a Radical Digital Humanism. It is based on the general principles of Digital Humanism that are concretised and combined with the critical analysis of digital exploitation and digital domination as well as the insight that democratic socialism is the type of society that helps to practically realise Humanism. The implication is that we need democratic digital socialism to practically realise Digital Humanism.

Radical Digital Humanism is a materialist philosophy that stresses the productive, social and transformative capacities of human beings that enable them to liberate themselves from digital class society, digital capitalism, digital exploitation, digital domination, digital ideology and to together create a better world. It has three dimensions:

- *Radical Digital Humanism's Epistemology: Critical Digital Research and Thought*
  Digital machines can and should not replace the human being. In a class society, such endeavours can result in the creation of digital fascism and digital barbarism. Given that computer technologies and machines in general are different from humans, big data-based, computational and digital methods can easily result in a digital positivism that destroys critical thinking and the social sciences and humanities by advancing instrumental reason. We need epistemologies, ways of thinking and research approaches that enable us to think critically about and critically analyse the digital and to develop and use critical theories of the digital, critical digital methods and critical digital ethics. Dialectical thinking is of high importance for such approaches. Computers are deterministic, undialectical machines that cannot replace and simulate the critical and dialectical thinking that humans are capable of.
- *Radical Digital Humanism's Ontology: The Human as Social, Societal, Producing Being*
  Technologies in general and computers in particular are not human, social and societal beings. Human beings and their activities, social relations and connections constitute society. In contemporary societies digital technologies shape and are shaped by humans and their social relations, but such technologies are not autonomous actors and are

different from humans, which is why digital machines should not be analysed as if they were humans and humans should not be analysed as if they were machines.
The activities, social relations and social production processes of humans constitute society and digital society. Technological determinism is an ideology that proclaims that machines in general and digital machines in particular are autonomous from humans and change society. In contrast, Radical Digital Humanism stresses that there is a dialectic of society and digital technologies, which means that humans and their social relations shape, design and use digital technologies that have complex dynamics that can result in unpredictable consequences and impacts. Digital technologies often do not have one single form of use and single impacts, but multiple, contradictory and antagonistic uses and impacts that are embedded into society's contradictions and antagonisms. Radical Digital Humanism critically analyses alienation, exploitation and domination, and their interactions in the context of digitalisation and digital technologies. This includes the critical analysis of capitalism, class, patriarchy, racism, dictatorship, ideology, disrespect, the interactions of these phenomena, as well as the analysis of praxis and social struggles in the context of the digital.

- *Radical Digital Humanism's Axiology: The Philosophy of Digital Praxis*
  Radical Digital Humanism's ethics is a praxis philosophy that critically analyses digital alienation, digital exploitation, digital domination, digital ideology as well as social struggles that oppose these processes. Radical Digital Humanism critically analyses and opposes the reduction of humans and society to the status of machines. It is a critique of instrumental reason and reification in the digital age.

> Radical Digital Humanism argues that it is not enough to critically analyse the digital world but that as long as exploitation and domination exist, the point is to change it. Therefore, Radical Digital Humanism as praxis philosophy wants to create critical knowledge that can inform struggles and processes that lead to a humane digital society where all humans lead a good life, flourish and can realise their potentials, where everyone benefits, and digital technologies are used for advancing wealth for all; the abolishment, minimisation and reduction of toil; participatory democracy; and the cultural commons. In a nutshell, Radical Digital Humanism is the creation of knowledge about the digital and digital technologies that support the advancement of democratic socialism and digital socialism (see Fuchs 2020b). Radical Digital Humanism's ethics is an ethics of class and social struggles. Convinced that humans deserve and need a society that benefits all, it argues that it is worth and necessary that humans struggle for and engage in praxis that aims at digital socialism.

Radical Digital Humanism is a materialist approach to the study of, reflection on, and development of digital technologies and digital society that is focused on the need of humans to liberate themselves from digital class society, digital exploitation, digital domination and digital ideology, and to together create a good digital society. Radical Digital Humanism stands in the tradition of both Humanism and Radical Humanism. It is Radical Humanism in and for the digital age. In order to circumvent society gliding into disaster, destruction and annihilation, Radical Digital Humanism sees the need of all humanists of the world to unite and form a front against fascism and inhumanity, including digital fascism and digital inhumanity. Radical Digital Humanism is an open approach interested in co-operation and forging alliances to save humanity and society in the digital age from barbarism.

In the next section, we will discuss some objections to Digital Humanism.

4. OBJECTIONS TO DIGITAL HUMANISM

Structuralists will argue that Digital Humanism is too much focused on the individual in the digital age and does not give enough attention to how digital structures shape, constrain and dominate individuals. Digital Humanists should answer to Structuralists that the human being is also in the digital age as a social and societal being which means that there are dialectics of subjects and objects, individuals and society, practices and structures, society and technology that are mediated by the digital.

Some Post-structuralists will argue that Digital Humanism is yet another truth claim and grand narrative and therefore a form of totalitarianism. Digital Humanists should answer to Post-structuralists that the assumption that there is no truth and no universality contributed to the emergence of digital post-truth culture, 'fake news', relativism, the fragmentation and polarisation of digital society. Digital Humanists should ascertain that it is important that we hold on to and renew the ideas of truth, the common, the human being, democracy and universal rights in the digital age.

Some Post-humanists will argue that Digital Humanism overestimates the positive capacities of the human being, underestimates the agency of non-humans and the emancipatory potentials of cyborgs, and ignores the destructive actions of humans. Digital Humanists should answer to Post-humanists that humans are not machines, that there are dialectics of humans and machines in society, that the equalisation of humans and machines advances instrumental reason, that instrumental reason has fascist potentials, and that humans are not as such destructive but are turned into destructors in alienated societies, which means we do not have to abolish humans but alienation.

Some Post-colonialists will argue that Humanism has advanced racism, white supremacy, Eurocentrism and Western-centrism, and that Digital Humanism faces the danger of being a racist, supremacist, Eurocentric and Western-centric project. Digital Humanists should answer to Post-colonialists that they too oppose racism, that particularisms that limit rights and universality to certain groups are no Humanisms at all, that Digital Humanism stresses the common aspects and rights of all humans in digital society, that Humanism has historically existed in many different versions in all parts of the world and that we need to and should build on the rich history of Humanism, engage with its variety of versions. Digital Humanism should be approached in transcultural and transdisciplinary manners.

Some environmentalists and critics of anthropocentrism who stress the concept of the Anthropocene and related ideas will argue that Digital Humanism underestimates how humans have destroyed nature and that there is the danger that Digital Humanism will advance unsustainable forms of digital technologies that humans use to treat nature as an enemy that is conquered and destroyed. Digital Humanists should answer to critics of anthropocentrism that it is not an abstract humanity that has created the environmental crisis, but that rather than the Anthropocene it is the Capitalocene that has unleashed destructive forces that have destructed nature and alienated humans and society. Digital Humanism includes digital environmental ethics that argues for the sustainable organisation of the relationship between humans and nature in the digital age.

Some feminists and gender equality activists will argue that Humanism has historically turned into an ideology that limited humanity to men and denied humanity to women, other genders, people of colour etc., and that Digital Humanism faces the danger of reproducing this ideology in the digital age. Digital Humanists should reply to feminists and gender equality activists that gender-based oppression, racism and classism are not Humanist because Humanism focuses on what all humans have in common and does not want to divide humanity. Digital Humanism is interested in overcoming inequalities having to do with class, gender, racism and the intersections of oppression.

Some Socialists will argue that Humanism has historically resulted in possessive individualism that has benefited the ruling class and has justified the exploitation and expropriation of the working class. They will say that therefore there is the danger that Digital Humanism is a liberal project that serves and justifies the interests of the capitalist class in the digital age. Digital Humanists should answer to socialists that there has been a rich variety of Humanisms, including Socialist Humanism. They should say that in the contemporary digital age we need a renewal of Socialist Humanism and that the greatest danger humanity faces today is a new fascism. A united front of the world's Humanists, including socialist, progressive and liberal Humanists, is needed in order to advance democracy and anti-fascism. Contemporary liberals should be reminded that neoliberalism has backfired and advanced fascist potentials and realities, which is why liberalism needs to renew itself and commit to the advancement of the social good.

Some conservatives will argue that Digital Humanism makes the universalist claims that all humans are equal, that in reality humans are unequal and that as a consequence, inequalities in the digital age are not a problem because everyone can improve their position in society by performance and hard work. Digital Humanists should answer to conservatives that inequalities do not exist by nature and are in digital society just like in previous epochs socially produced. They should give examples of how the winners of digital society have not become wealthy, powerful and influential by hard labour but because of inheritance, class relations, political and ideological affiliation, and chance. Digital Humanists should engage in dialogue with digital conservatives in order to avoid the advancement of filter bubbles, echo chambers and polarisation.

Fascists will argue that Digital Humanism is an elitist, metropolitan project that does not speak to everyday people, undermines the nation and embraces foreign cultures which will result in the decline of the West and the downfall of the Occident and civilisation. Fascists call for the organisation of the survival of the fittest and all-out war in digital society. Digital Humanists should answer to fascists that the separation of humanity into friends and enemies is an ideological project that serves dominant interests and distracts from the real causes of the problems society faces in the digital age. They should show how the very ideology and contradictions of fascism in the digital age mean disadvantages for everyday people as well as the support and masking of dominant interests. The Humanist alternative is to stress what humans have in common and what unites them and that in a global, digital and pandemic age, global problems can only be solved by international co-operation and are worsened by nationalist projects. Digital Humanists should point out that the logic of the friend/enemy scheme has historically resulted in wars and that wars kill and harm everyday people.

5. CONCLUSION

This chapter asked: What is Digital Humanism? For giving an answer, minimum definitions of Humanism and Digital Humanisms were established that have three dimensions (epistemology, ontology, axiology). Humanism is a philosophical approach that stresses the active and transformative capacities of human beings in the social world. Digital Humanism is a philosophical approach that stresses the active and transformative capacities of human beings in the digital age.

This chapter argued for Radical Digital Humanism. Radical/Socialist Humanism is a materialist philosophy that stresses the productive, social and transformative capacities of human beings that enable them to liberate themselves from class society, capitalism, exploitation, domination and ideology and to together create a better world. Radical Digital Humanism is a materialist approach to the study of, reflection on, and development of digital technologies and digital society that is focused on the need of humans to liberate themselves from digital class society, digital capitalism, digital exploitation, digital domination and digital ideology and to together create a good digital society. Radical Digital Humanism stands in the tradition of both Humanism and Radical Humanism. It is Radical Humanism in and for the digital age.

This chapter stresses the need for the collaboration of contemporary Humanisms and Digital Humanisms in order to fight against fascism and circumvent the collapse of society and humanity.

The digital mediates not all, but many aspects of everyday life today. Digital Humanism is a contribution to digital ethics. Given the global problems societies and humanity face today, we urgently need to ask moral questions: What is a good society? What is a good digital society? What needs to be done so that we establish a good digital society? What have been the major factors that have prevented the establishment of a good society? What should we do in order to advance a good digital society? Digital Humanism is a philosophical approach that helps us to reflect on these questions. In the age of inhumanity, we need to renew Humanism. We need Radical Humanism. We need Radical Digital Humanism.

4

DE-COLONISING ACADEMIA: A RADICAL HUMANIST PERSPECTIVE

1. INTRODUCTION

Since more than two decades, there have been calls for and attempts to make the voices and knowledge of non-Western scholars more heard and visible in academia. More recently, these attempts have been presented under the label of 'de-colonising' research and teaching. There have been calls for de-colonising the mind, the university, knowledge and the curriculum (e.g. Begum and Saini 2019; Bhambra, Gebrial and Nişancıoğlu 2018; Grosfoguel, Hernández and Velásquez 2016; Le Grange 2016; Mbembe 2016, 2015; Ngũgĩ,1986; Santos 2017, 2019).

This essay is a reflection on the de-colonisation of academia and the study of the media, communication and the digital. It asks: what does it mean to de-colonise academia and the study of media, communication and the digital? How can academia be transformed in progressive ways?

This chapter takes a Radical Humanist and Political Economy perspective on de-colonisation, which means that it is interested in how capitalism, power and material aspects of academia such as resources, money, infrastructures, time, space, working conditions and social relations of production shape the possibilities and realities of research and teaching (see Fuchs 2020c, Mosco 2009, Murdock and Golding 2005).

Section 2 discusses some aspects of the attempts to de-colonise the study of media, communication and the digital. When we talk about the de-colonisation of academia, we need a proper understanding and a definition of de-colonisation. Section 3 provides a political economy understanding of (de-) colonisation. It asks: what is (neo-)colonialism? Based on Section 3's understanding of neo-colonialism, Section 4 discusses the colonisation of academia from a political economy perspective. Section 5 draws conclusion and discusses what changes are needed in order to progressively transform academia in general and the field of Media and Communication Studies in particular.

2. DE-COLONISATION IN THE STUDY OF MEDIA, COMMUNICATION AND THE DIGITAL

Just like in other fields of studies, also in Media and Communication Studies and Digital Research, labels such as 'de-Westernising', 'internationalisation', 'globalisation', 'de-colonisation' and '(de)provincialisation' have been used for pointing towards the lack of visibility of scholars, approaches, academic knowledge, texts, theories and methods from Africa and the Global South and arguing for changes (see, e.g. Chakravartty, Kuo, Grubbs and McIlwain 2018; Curran and Park 2000; Dutta 2020; Fuchs and Qiu 2018; Kraidy 2018; Kumar and Parameswaran 2018; Makoni and Masters 2021; Shome 2016; Sparks 2018; Thussu 2009; Waisbord and

Mellado 2014; Wang 2011; Willems 2014; Willems and Mano 2016). Thus far, de-Westernisation has primarily meant that Western universities have discovered the Global South as an educational market and that in the realm of the media industry, media and tech companies have discovered the Global South as a realm of consumer culture (see milton and Mano, 2021, 258).

Given that such calls have over two decades not brought about substantial changes, Winston Mano and viola c. milton argue for an Afrokology of Media and Communication Studies (Mano and milton, 2021, milton and Mano, 2021), which means 'recognising the importance of African insight and knowledge in thinking about media and communication' (milton and Mano, 2021, 258) and 'views from Africa' that 'open up the field and offer new ways of thinking about issues that tend to be overlooked or conceptualised differently in dominant academic circles' (milton and Mano, 2021, 259). 'The study of media and communications in the global South is limited by uncritical overreliance on theories and methodologies from the global North' (milton and Mano, 2021, 256). They take the works of Molefi Kete Asante (Asante and Ledbetter 2016), Dani Wadada Nabudere (2006, 2011, 2012) and Francis B. Nyamnjoh (2017, 2020) as starting points. In a more general sense, de-colonisation of academia means 'to embrace a pluriverse of Southern values, perspectives and societies to understand the coexisting epistemologies and practices of the different worlds and problems we inhabit and encounter' (milton and Mano, 2021, 260). Generalising this approach of an Afrokology of Media and Communication Studies means, based on Boaventura de Sousa Santos (2016, 2017, 2018), epistemologies of the South in Media and Communication Studies that are anchored in the experiences of social groups 'that have systematically suffered injustice, oppression and destruction caused by capitalism, colonialism and patriarchy' (Santos 2017, 150).

2.1 Trans-Disciplinarity

Based on Ivan Illich (1975) and Francis B. Nyamnjoh (2017, 2020), Mano and milton characterise such an Afrokology and epistemologies of the South as convivial and trans-disciplinary. They argue that scholars from the Global South's approaches, knowledge, texts, theories and methods should be much more recognised in the academic discourse as equals so that intercultural conversations, dialogue and cooperation are enabled that result in trans-disciplinary research. 'Afrokology deployed in this way explores how the field of Media and Communication Studies can embrace a relational theoretical and methodological episteme. Such an epistemological turn would make explicit the issue of praxis, i.e. listening and learning from others in any development towards meaningful engagement with realities in Africa' (Mano and milton, 2021, 37).

Transcending boundaries in research is an important and promising idea. Within capitalism, trans-disciplinarity is, however, prone to ideological abuse. Conservative forces often present established academic fields and disciplines as ivory towers of knowledge that are detached from 'real life' in order to argue that research should do something 'useful' that benefits capitalist companies and/or governments. Trans-disciplinarity is then often employed as a label for advancing an agenda that undermines the independence of research and wants to turn it into instrumental reason and instrumental knowledge production. The buzzwords of inter-, cross- and trans-disciplinarity are furthermore often used for promoting the colonisation of research and academia by particular approaches, especially business and management studies, the natural sciences, and computer science. Such understandings of trans-disciplinarity threaten the autonomy and role of critique, critical reflection and critical knowledge production in the social sciences and humanities and advance new forms of positivism. We therefore need critical trans-disciplinarity.

True trans-disciplinarity is guided by human interests and transcends disciplines by asking and analysing big questions about the world and society in critical manners that create academic knowledge that helps to advance a good society, which requires to bring together and transcend different approaches, actors and specialisms. Media and communication studies is as such inter- and trans-disciplinary because communication exists in all realms of society. Therefore, analysing communication requires that communication scholars not just acquire skills in distinct Media and Communication Research approaches and theories but also in skills from other academic fields. The Political Economy of Communication is an inherently trans-disciplinary approach that transcends the boundaries between and brings together the social sciences and humanities, empirical research and theory, research and praxis; political science, economics and moral philosophy/ethics. A good trans-disciplinary researcher understands and uses Political Economy.

2.2 Pluriversality as Unity in Plurality

Mano and milton suggest 'African-driven approaches that are recognisable as such', 'the dialogue between particularity and universality within a pluriversal context' and 'creating space for African-driven theories and approaches to travel without losing their radical edge' (Mano and milton 2021, 21). They argue that African approaches to Media and Communication Studies 'can work independently' (22) and have value in themselves as 'independent and meaningful categories on their own terms that produce an epistemic shift based on African lived experiences' (23).

Pluriversal approaches do not automatically argue for isolation, dualism and difference without unity but for interaction and engagement with existing knowledge and approaches. We 'redeploy Afrokology as a decolonial heuristic tool that tactically mobilises African heritage such as *ubuntu*, *ujaama*, *humanism*, *maat*, *sankofa* to uncover epistemological frameworks as part of a strategic turn to the core preoccupation with what it means to be African and human today' (Mano and milton, 2021, 24). Mano and milton argue for the affirmation of 'the diversity, and multiple experiences, dialectics and geographies' of Africa in 'a world community' (26), where African knowledge is not 'a suppressed category or appendage' (28).

Mano and milton (2021) take Dani Wadada Nabudere's (2006) understanding of Afrokology as their starting point:

> Afrokology is *'not necessarily African-centric or Afrocentric. It is a universal scientific epistemology that goes beyond Eurocentricism, or other ethnocentrisms. It recognises all sources of knowledge as valid within their historical, cultural or social contexts and seeks to engage them into a dialogue that can lead to better knowledge for all. […] Afrokology must proceed from the proposition that it is a true philosophy of knowledge and wisdom based on African cosmogonies because it is* Afro- *in that it is inspired by the ideas originally produced from the Cradle of Humankind located in Africa.* It is not Afrikology because it is African *but it is* Afro-

> *because it emanates from the source of the universal system of knowledge in Africa. The product is therefore not relativistic to Africa but universalistic with its base in Africa. It is* -(ko)logy *because it is based on* logos – *the word from which the universe arose. From the word emerged consciousness and from consciousness emerged humanity who produced language and script from the word. Afrokology draws its scientificity and uniqueness from the fact that it is based on an all-embracing philosophy of humankind originating in Egypt and updated by the lived experiences of all humanity, who still continue to draw on its deep-rooted wisdom'.*
>
> (Nabudere 2006, 9, 20)

Mano and milton (2021) argue that Nabudere's approach focuses 'on a singular source of knowledge production (i.e. "tradition" and "African knowledge") that negates diversity', idealises 'Africa's "glorious" past', advances an 'uncritical and romanticised embrace of the African past' and is too much focused on 'the collective authorship of African knowledge, at the expense of individual creativity' (Mano and milton, 2021, 31). The authors utilise the notion of the pluriverse.

By the term the pluriverse, Arturo Escobar (2018, xvi) refers to '*a world where many worlds fit*'. Boaventura de Sousa Santos (2018, 216) argues for a 'radical or ontological pluralism (a multiverse or pluriverse rather than the universe) and of a multiplicity of viewpoints, the notion that truth and reality are perceived differently from diverse points of view, and that no single point of view is the complete truth'. 'The work of the epistemologies of the South consists of evaluating the relative reasonableness and adequateness of the different kinds of knowledge in light of the social struggles in which the relevant epistemic community is involved' (Santos 2018, 39). Building on Escobar, Amaya Querejazu argues: 'Taking the pluriverse as an ontological starting point, implies not simply tolerating difference, but actually understanding that reality is constituted not only by many worlds, but by many kinds of worlds, many ontologies, many ways of being in the world, many ways of knowing reality, and experimenting those many worlds [...] Drawing from other worldviews – mainly indigenous relational worldviews –, the pluriverse implies the existence of many worlds somehow interconnected' (Querejazu 2016, 13).

Mano and milton situate the notion of the pluriverse in the context of Media and Communication Studies. 'Importantly, "de-provincialising" [indiginous epistemes] underscores the decolonial objective of "de-universalising" knowledge' (Mano and milton, 2021, 23). 'Afrokology rejects universality in favour of "pluriversality"' (Mano and milton, 2021, 25). 'We are not in search of universality, opting instead for pluriversality' (Mano and milton, 2021, 32), understood as 'a need to consider how different worlds can coexist, not submitted in one reality, but in incommensurability' (Querejazu 2016, 2). The pluriverse 'includes modern Western ontologies, which complement and are interconnected, or better said, partially connected with the other world of other cosmovisions' (Querejazu 2016, 13).

Based on the notion of the pluriverse and Nyamnjoh's works (2017, 2020), Mano and milton argue for convivial scholarship that does not throw away Western knowledge but enters into a conversation and dialogue among equals with its representatives which creates 'relational epistemologies' (Mano and milton, 2021, 33), avoids 'insular particularity' (34) and creates '*critical* particularity' (34).

Cultural imperialism is a unity without diversity that privileges and imposes the repressive culture originating in one part of the world on other parts of the world. Reversing dominance so that a new unity without diversity is established or struggles for separation, that is, diversity without unity, fetishises either singularly defined universality (unity without diversity) or independent singularities (diversity without unity). The result is cultural domination on the one hand and cultural fragmentation on the other hand. Unity without diversity creates and sustains a public sphere that excludes certain parts of the world and is thereby incomplete. Diversity without unity creates local, fragmented, micro public spheres where humans and cultures are just seen as being different and do not engage in communication and solidarity. Such fragmented publics discourage sharing and that humans perceive themselves as having something in common and doing something together. Postmodern approaches have stressed diversity, plurality and difference without unity.

Unity in diversity and in plurality stands in contrast to plurality without unity and unity without plurality. It is a dialectic of the common and differences, a dialectic of unity and diversity. Unity in diversity means approaches that focus on identifying the common aspects of and bringing together different humans and approaches. It focuses on what humans have in common and what unites them besides all their differences. Such approaches look for the universal in the particular; they do not want to de-universalise but to make the unseen, the unknown and the invisible part of the universal. We are all human beings striving for happiness and a good social life, which is why full independence of one knowledge and existence from all others is not possible, not desirable and not meaningful. One needs some form of universality; otherwise, communication is not possible and isolation, fragmentation, separatism and hostility are the consequence. In academia, we need to recognise and acknowledge that there are different starting points and entry points into the creation of knowledge that reflect specific experiences, situations, worldviews and circumstances and that when entering into dialogue can show the commonalities of humans and why and that they together form humanity. The de-colonisation of knowledge should be an 'invasion into universality' (Sartre 1963, 13), an invasion into the quest for creating unity in diversity of knowledge. I therefore want to understand pluri-versality as a struggle for universality with different entry and starting points that bring together, share, unite and create the common of different perspectives, experiences and knowledge.

2.3 Conviviality

Consequently, milton and Mano (2021) argue for Afrokology as trans-disciplinary heuristic and toolkit that supports cooperation of scholars from different academic fields, cooperation of academics and non-academics, the combination of research and praxis, asking questions, conducting research and creating knowledge that provide 'answers to problems previously outside of the scope of the field' and help advancing social justice, empowerment and freedom (milton and Mano, 2021, 265), establishing a 'methodology of the oppressed', 'developing an ethics of relational accountability that promotes respectful representation, reciprocity, and rights of the researched' and 'relexicalising the field, including for example reinterpretation of the work of major Euro-American theorists in relation to the insights of those African experiences that insist on international solidarity and resistance to racism, gender and class bias' (milton and Mano, 2021, 272). Trans-disciplinarity 'engenders a new culture based on convergence between disciplines that generates new knowledge, methods and approaches' (milton and Mano, 2021, 263).

Advancing knowledge in, from and about the Global South is not enough. For example, the reproduction of the neoliberal logic of the Western business school and the kind of knowledge it produces in the Global South, that is, the creation of business schools in the Global South that aim at advancing capitalism in the Global South, does not help human emancipation. The point of de-colonising knowledge is therefore the advancement of critical knowledge about the world, which must include knowledge in, from and about the Global South. The de-colonisation of academia requires a material infrastructure of research and higher education.

The word 'convivial' goes etymologically back to the Latin term *convivium*, which means a feast and the Latin word *convivialis* (Hoad 1996, 96), which means 'pertaining to a feast' (Online Etymology Dictionary 2021). It was introduced to the English language in the 1660s. Conviviality means and includes friendliness, liveliness and togetherness. Changing academia and society in a positive manner cannot be achieved individually but requires that academics come together and collectively transform dominant structures.

According to Francis B. Nyamnjoh (2002), conviviality involves agents in 'good company where enmity and gloom have no place' (111), 'the spirit of togetherness, interpenetration and intersubjectivity' (111–112). Conviviality thus stresses 'empowerment for individuals and groups alike, and not the marginalisation of the one by or for the other' (112). Nyamnjoh (2017, 262) argues that conviviality involves the insight that we and the world are incomplete and that by reaching out to others, we learn from them and establish 'prospects for mutual gain' (265). 'Conviviality offers spaces and opportunities for mutually edifying conversations across various divides, hierarchies and inequalities. [...] It is in this sense that one can imagine and promote an infinite number of conviviality spaces – political, cultural, religious, economic, gender, class, generational, geographical, etc. – all stressing interconnections, dialogue, collaboration, interdependence and compassion. It is about building bridges and linking people, spaces and places, cross-fertilising ideas, and inspiring imagination and innovative ways of seeking and consolidating the good life for all and sundry' (266). Convivial scholarship is 'a critical scholarship of recognition and reconciliation' (267) that 'recognises the deep power of collective imagination and the importance of interconnections and nuanced complexities' (268).

Nyamnjoh envisions progressive transformation of academia, a concrete utopia of a better university and better academia in a good society. It becomes evident from his writing that conviviality is about three Cs: (re)*c*ognising others, *c*ommunicating with others and *c*ooperating with others (see also Hofkirchner 2009). The reality of academia and society often looks different. These spheres of existence are shaped by competition, accumulation, instrumentalisation, commodification and alienation. Conviviality is an ideal we need to struggle for. Convivial scholarship exists partly today, but academia is also confronted by and widely shaped by the forces of competition, accumulation, instrumentalisation, commodification and alienation. Conviviality requires material foundations that enable and give humans access to the time, space and resources that are preconditions for practising conviviality.

In the 1970s, Ivan Illich's (1975) book *Tools for Conviviality* introduced the notion of conviviality to the academic and political discourse.

'Such a society, in which modern technologies serve politically interrelated individuals rather than managers, I will call "convivial"', a 'modern society of responsibly limited tools' (Illich 1975, 12). The notion of conviviality has played a role in the philosophy and ethics of technology. It is based on the insight that not everything that is technologically possible is morally desirable. In class societies, many technologies do not advance the public good, but only serve the particularistic interests of some, are destructive technologies that harm humans, society and nature, or advance exploitation and domination. Illich argues that we should responsibly limit the realisation of technological possibilities to those options that benefit all.

But conviviality goes beyond technology. Illich has a broad understanding of tools. He understands tools not just as machines, but as 'productive institutions' that also produce goods such as education, health, knowledge or decisions (34). In a convivial society and convivial social systems, humans come together freely, guided by friendliness and joyfulness, in order to cooperate so that products emerge that are common goods and serve the public good. A convivial society is the 'autonomous and creative intercourse among persons, and the intercourse of persons with their environment' (24) that benefits all, which is why Illich speaks of 'a convivial mode of production' and the 'convivial commonweal' (29). In convivial academia, scholars come together to create critical knowledge that helps advance the common good that benefits all.

Illich was a critic of both capitalist and Stalinist societies. Both types of social systems lead to 'specialization of functions, institutionalization of values and centralization of power and turns people into the accessories of bureaucracies or machines' (12). Illich did not see Stalinist societies as forms of socialism. He argued for 'participatory socialism' (122), that is, socialist democracy and democratic socialism. 'The transition to socialism cannot be affected without an inversion of our present institutions and the substitution of convivial for industrial tools. At the same time, the retooling of society will remain a pious dream unless the ideals of socialist justice prevail' (25). Convivial technologies and structures are part of the creation of democratic socialism.

Conviviality is not simply a mindset, an attitude, a worldview, a moral principle or individual behaviour. It is much more than that. It is a type of social system, a way of designing and shaping society. Conviviality includes 'the triadic relationship between persons, tools, and a new collectivity' (12). Attaining convivial academia is a question of changing social relations, power structures and political economy so that humans can come together and produce social relations, knowledge and tools that help advancing the public good.

Calls for de-colonising and de-Westernising academia and Media and Communication Studies have been calls for trans-disciplinarity, pluriversality and conviviality. I have argued that these notions have certain limits and should therefore be understood as critical trans-disciplinarity, the struggle for unity in diversity, and changes of social relations, power structures and political economy. This means de-colonisation is a material process. In this context, the question arises what (neo-)colonialism actually means. The next section deals with this question.

3. WHAT IS (NEO-)COLONIALISM?

When discussing 'de-colonisation', one needs understandings and definitions of colonialism and neo-colonialism. Marxist theory has prominently featured the notions of the colony and colonialism. We will therefore discuss some relevant approaches that take Marx as their starting point in order to provide an understanding of colonialism and contemporary neo-colonialism.

3.1 Classical Colonialism

Classical colonialism was the violent appropriation of land, labour power, nature, raw materials, women and the creation of international markets. It resulted in the division of power and labour between empires and colonies. Colonialism is the violent search for and appropriation of gratis and cheap means of production and gratis and cheap labour. Colonialism makes use of the military, state administration and managerial services 'to discover the wealth of the [colonised] country, to extract it and to send it off to the mother countries. [...] The wealth of the imperial countries is our [the colonised's] wealth too. [...] Europe is literally the creation of the Third World. The wealth which smothers her is that which was stolen from the under developed peoples' (Fanon 1963, 102). Militarism and war play a key role in classical colonialism:

> *...the weakest states are those we call colonies, by which we mean administrative units that are defined as non-sovereign and fall under the jurisdiction of another state, normally distant from it. The origin of modern colonies is in the economic expansion of the world-system. In this expansion, strong states at the core tried to incorporate new zones into the processes of the modern world-system. [...] the colonial powers justified their assumption of authority and the distribution of roles to persons from the 'metropolitan' country by a combination of arguments: racist arguments about the cultural inferiority and inadequacy of the local populations; and self-justifying arguments about the 'civilizing' role the colonial administration was performing. [...] one of the objectives of the colonizing power was not*

merely to ensure its control of the production processes in the colony but also to make sure that no other relatively strong state in the world-system could have access to the resources or the markets of the colony, or at most minimal access
(Wallerstein 2004, 55–56)

Militarism fulfils a quite definite function in the history of capital, accompanying as it does every historical phase of accumulation. It plays a decisive part in the first stages of European capitalism, in the period of the so-called 'primitive accumulation', as a means of conquering the New World and the spice-producing countries of India. Later, it is employed to subject the modern colonies, to destroy the social organisations of primitive societies so that their means of production may be appropriated, forcibly to introduce commodity trade in countries where the social structure had been unfavourable to it, and to turn the natives into a proletariat by compelling them to work for wages in the colonies. It is responsible for the creation and expansion of spheres of interest for European capital in non-European regions, for extorting railway concessions in backward countries, and for enforcing the claims of European capital as international lender. Finally, militarism is a weapon in the competitive struggle between capitalist countries for areas of non-capitalist civilisation
(Luxemburg 1913/2003, 434)

3.2 Colonialism and Racism

Colonialism has at the ideological level been closely aligned with racism as ideology that makes and diffuses the claim that certain groups are biologically and culturally inferior in order to justify their exploitation and domination. Racism is an ideology used for justifying and enforcing class society. Racism dehumanises humans ideologically by declaring them to be subhuman and inferior humans and ideologically reducing them to the status of things (reification). Racism and colonialism are laying 'claim to and denying the human condition at the same time [...] Chatter, chatter: liberty, equality, fraternity, love, honor, patriotism, and what have you. All this did not prevent us from making anti-racial speeches about dirty niggers, dirty Jews, and dirty Arabs' (Sartre 1963, 20, 26). Classical colonialism is 'racist humanism' (Sartre 1963, 26) that undermines Humanism by advancing a particularist notion of the human that denies certain groups being human. 'Racism is *already there*, carried by the *praxis* of colonialism, engendered at every instant by the colonial apparatus, sustained by those relationships of production which define two sorts of individuals' (Sartre 1964/2001, 21). Racism is not just an anti-Humanist ideology, but also an anti-Humanist practice of racially motivated exploitation and domination that subjects certain humans to violence, the (super-)exploitation of their labour, exclusion and control based on and in order to advance racist ideology (see Balibar and Wallerstein 1991).

Colonialism, including the conquest of foreign territories and slavery, was a condition for the transition from feudalism to capitalism. 'In 1492 the characteristics of pre-industrial capitalism were already in Europe, as they were in some other areas. But this mode of production was dominant only over small sections of the European landscape, and it did not have behind it the force power. So it could not accumulate capital, increase production, increase the wage-work force, etc., very quickly. Colonialism removed the constraints. It provided capitalism in this region with the resources needed to increase its scale and increase its political power' (Blaut 1989, 290).

Slavery was part of the colonial mechanisms that enabled the rise of capitalism. The rise of capitalism required the 'colonial slave regimes of the modern Europeans' where, among others, 'more than 11.5 million Africans [were] transported to the slave regimes of the Americas' (Patterson 1982, 118). 'The vast majority of Africans brought to the New World were not prisoners taken in, wars either of their own making or of anyone else's. As Equiano and other African ex-slaves who wrote their autobiographies so often insisted, the slaves were stolen from their homes by European-supported thieves' (Patterson 1982, 122).

3.3 Colonies and Ongoing Primitive Accumulation

For the classical thinkers of imperialism, imperialism meant the combination of finance capital, the monopolisation of capital, capital export and the military competition for spheres and territories of influence and accumulation.

For Rosa Luxemburg, imperialism is a further development of colonialism. It is a form of capitalism that makes use of ongoing primitive accumulation, that is, the subsumption of non-capitalist spheres of life under capitalism with a variety of means. 'Non-capitalist organisations provide a fertile soil for capitalism; more strictly: capital feeds on the ruins of such organisations, and although this non-capitalist *milieu* is indispensable for accumulation, the latter proceeds at the cost of this medium nevertheless, by eating it up. [...] Only the continuous and progressive disintegration of non-capitalist organisations makes accumulation of capital possible' (Luxemburg 1913/2003, 397). 'Rosa Luxemburg showed that historically such a system never existed, that capitalism had always needed what she called "non-capitalist milieux and strata" for the extension of labour force, resources and above all the extension of markets. These non-capitalist milieux and strata were initially the peasants and artisans with their "natural economy", later the colonies. Colonialism for Rosa Luxemburg is therefore not only the last stage of capitalism [...], but its constant necessary condition. In other words, without colonies capital accumulation or extended reproduction of capital would come to a stop' (Mies 1986, 34).

Maria Mies (1986) used Luxemburg's notion of ongoing primitive accumulation for arguing that capitalism requires and creates 'internal and external colonies', 'the housewives in the industrialized countries and the colonies in Africa, Asia and Latin America' (Mies 1986, 17). She extended Luxemburg's approach for arguing that there is a distinct link of capitalism, patriarchy and colonialism so that capital not just exploits wage workers, but also workers in the colonies and women as houseworkers whose reproductive labour reproduces labour power without payment. In neoliberal capitalism, more and more humans would be turned into precarious workers who face conditions that houseworkers have always faced in capitalism, namely 'unrestricted exploitation and superexploitation' (Mies 1986, 123). This includes, for example, turning wage workers and houseworkers into small entrepreneurs (Mies 1986, 123). Mies characterises neoliberalism as a form of neo-colonialism where lots of humans are turned into precarious, housework-like labourers (housewifisation).

In a way comparable to Maria Mies, David Harvey argues that global, neoliberal capitalism is a form of ongoing primitive accumulation that he terms accumulation by dispossession.

> *What accumulation by dispossession does is to release a set of assets (including labour power) at very low (and in some instances zero) cost.*
>
> (Harvey 2003, 149)

> *Accumulation by dispossession became increasingly more salient after 1973, in part as compensation for the chronic problems of overaccumulation arising within expanded reproduction. The primary vehicle for this development was financialization and the orchestration, largely at the behest of the United States, of an inter national financial system that could, from time to time, visit anything from mild to savage bouts of devaluation and accumulation by dispossession on certain sectors or even whole territories. [...] The rise of neo-liberal theory and its associated politics of privatization symbolized much of what this shift was about.*
>
> (Harvey 2003, 156)

> *The primary vehicle for accumulation by dispossession, therefore, has been the forcing open of markets throughout the world by institutional pressures exercised through the IMF and the WTO, backed by the power of the United States (and to a lesser extent Europe) to deny access to its own vast market to those countries that refuse to dismantle their protections.*
>
> (Harvey 2003, 181)

The key processes of accumulation by dispossession are privatisation, commodification, financialisation, debt crises and state-organised redistribution from lower to upper classes (Harvey 2005, 160–164). The consequence is the commodification of (almost) everything, including education, higher education, research, knowledge, culture, the media, communication and technology. Accumulation by dispossession also includes the classical method of warfare in order to gain access to means of production such as land, raw materials such as oil, and labour power, as well as the transnationalisation of capital so that labour operates in a flexible manner globally and goes where it finds cheap labour that it can exploit.

3.4 Neo-Colonialism

Whereas classical colonialism and imperialism frequently worked with violence in the form of war, neo-colonialism often makes use of economic, non-violent political and ideological means: 'For the methods of neo-colonialists are subtle and varied. They operate not only in the economic field, but also in the political, religious, ideological and cultural spheres' (Nkrumah 1965, 239). 'Neo-colonialism is a modern form of colonialism. Actually, colonialism and neo-colonialism are the same thing; it is only in their form and in the way they exhibit themselves that they differ. Neo-colonialism is more disguised, more "modernized"' (FRELIMO 1965/1982, 4).

The creation of transnational corporations that exploit labour in the Global South in order to maximise their profits is an important aspect of neo-colonialism:

> *...the monopolies encourage 'runaway industries' in Third World countries in order to take advantage of cheap labour and tax incentives in these countries. [...] The transnational corporation secures this control over the raw material ventures and manufacturing joint ventures as well as the markets*

in the neo-colonial world through its control of technological know-how, management skills, and marketing link-ups throughout the world.

(Nabudere 1977, 250)

The essence of neo-colonialism is that the State which is subject to it is, in theory, independent and has all the outward trappings of international sovereignty. In reality its economic system and thus its political policy is directed from outside. [...] The result of neo-colonialism is that foreign capital is used for the exploitation rather than for the development of the less developed parts of the world. Investment under neo-colonialism increases rather than decreases the gap between the rich and the poor countries of the world.

(Nkrumah 1965, ix, x)

The colonial phase of the center-periphery division of labor corresponds logically to the first imperialist phase. Colonial and semicolonial dependent zones were relegated to the role of furnishers of raw materials to the industrial monopolies of the competing metropoles and of outlets for the noncompetitive industries which sustained the retrograde alliances in the metropoles. [...] The neocolonial phase corresponds to the reconstruction of the world market and the expansion of the multinationals.

(Amin 1980, 234–235)

Edward Said (2003, 352) therefore speaks of '"trans-national" neo-colonialism', which means that de-colonisation has been accompanied by recolonisation in the form of 'multinational capitalism and the [...] transnational corporations' (Jameson 1990, 47).

Nkrumah argues that capitalist control of the press and the media is one of the methods of neo-colonialism: 'While Hollywood takes care of fiction, the enormous monopoly press [...] attends to what it chooses to call "news"' (Nkrumah 1965, 246). The rise of neoliberal global capitalism has advanced the monopolisation of the capitalist media and tech sectors. For example, the Internet and digital technology are today dominated by a few platform capitalists such as Apple, Amazon, Google/Alphabet, Microsoft, Alibaba, Softbank, Facebook, Intel, IBM, Taiwan Semiconductor, Oracle, Cisco, Dell and Hon Hai Precision that are among the world's largest 100 transnational corporations (see Table 4.1).[1] In 2020, these 14 companies together had revenues of US$ 1.8 trillion. In 2020, the world's 33 poorest countries together had a gross domestic product of US$ 1.0 trillion.[2] The sales of the world's 14 largest digital corporations in 2020 was greater than the combined economic power of the world's 33 poorest countries in the Global South, which shows the tremendous economic power of monopoly capital.

3.5 From Classical Colonialism to Neo-Colonialism

Classical colonialism is the search for and practice of exploiting cheap and gratis labour and appropriating cheap and gratis resources and means of production from territories

1 Data source: Forbes 2000 List of the World's Biggest Public Companies, year 2021, https://www.forbes.com/lists/global2000/#1c92bc605ac0, accessed on 15 July 2021.

2 Data sources: United Nations 2020 (Human Development Index), World Development Indicators (GDO in current US$ for the year 2020 or the latest available year).

Table 4.1. The World's Largest Transnational Digital Corporations.

Position	Company	Country	Revenues 2020, in Billion US$
6	Apple	US	294
10	Amazon	US	381.6
13	Google/Alphabet	US	182.4
15	Microsoft	US	153.3
23	Alibaba Group	China	93.8
27	Softbank	Japan	61.8
33	Facebook	US	86
36	Intel	US	77.9
59	IBM	US	73.6
66	Taiwan Semiconductor	Taiwan	48.1
71	Oracle	US	39.7
75	Cisco Systems	US	48
92	Dell Technologies	US	94.3
94	Hon Hai Precision	Taiwan	182
			Total: 1,816.5

Source: Forbes 2000 List of the World's Biggest Public Companies, year 2021, https://www.forbes.com/lists/global2000/#1c92bc605ac0, accessed on 15 July 2021

that are conquered by violence and subdued with the help of racist ideology and state power, which also included slavery as violent appropriation of humans and the violent putting to work of their labour power.

Contemporary capitalism is neo-colonial in that it makes use of a variety of ways for creating colonies and extracting value from resources and exploiting labour in these colonies. Neo-colonialism means worldwide processes of ongoing primitive accumulation that partly work with violence, for example, the use of war for guaranteeing transnational corporations' access to oil, but also work with non-violent means such as transnational capital's export and activities, global monopoly capital, global commodification, privatisation, financialisation, debt crises, state-organised redistribution towards capital and the rich, culture, ideology, communication and the media. Neo-colonialism means talking about global capitalism. When talking about the de-colonisation of academia, we therefore need to talk about Political Economy and academic capitalism. The next section contributes to this task.

4. THE (DE-)COLONISATION OF ACADEMIA: A RADICAL HUMANIST AND POLITICAL ECONOMY PERSPECTIVE

4.1 The Neoliberal Colonisation of the University and Academia

Neoliberalism has also led to the global spread of capitalist ideology, including in universities worldwide, which has resulted in the dominance of the logic of the business school that is often the most influential and most well-resourced part of a university and spreads neoliberal ideology, that is, the idea that society should be organised and managed as spontaneous market order made up of the market activities of capitalist entrepreneurs. The logic of the business school has colonised the academic system and society, which has resulted in the privatisation of universities, the commodification of higher education programmes, the influence of for-profit corporations on research and higher education, the metrification of research and teaching, the running of universities by CEOs as businesses that consider students as 'customers' and academics as cost factors that need to be 'line-managed' as if they worked on an assembly line, etc.

Universities have thereby become more and more instrumentalised as direct creators of knowledge and skills that benefit and do not question capitalism and instrumental reason. Neo-colonialism has undermined the partial reality of universities as spheres of the creation of critical knowledge that deals with the complexity of the world's problems and critical thinking. The 'de-westernisation' of academia, including Media and Communication Studies, has in the context of neo-colonialism taken on an instrumental form, where Western universities educate tuition fee–paying students from all over the world in a higher education market that operates under neoliberal contexts.

The de-Westernisation of Media and Communication Studies in the past two decades has also meant that more academic knowledge has been produced, published and used that is focused on media and communication in the non-Western world and the Global South. This development as such should be welcome. Many academic works are today focused on the analysis and presentation of a single communication phenomenon in a single country. There are not enough studies that take an international comparative and transnational perspective. The reason is not simply that there is methodological nationalism that makes scholars and PhD researchers only interested in the country they were born in. Rather, conducting internationally comparative and transnational research is time-consuming and resource-intensive. It requires the cooperation of researchers and research teams in multiple countries. Research funding is predominantly nationalist and regionalist in character. It is largely focused on providing funding to researchers and enabling research time at the level of the nation-state and regional blocks of nation-states. There is very little international and global research funding available that allows researchers and research teams in multiple countries throughout the world to obtain significant amounts of funding that will allow them to dedicate significant amounts of time over a sustained period to trans-national and internationally comparative research. Trans-national and international research lacks the material preconditions of proper funding, infrastructures and resources. Research councils and governments follow nationalist research policy agendas that focus on developing national universities' research performance, their ranking in international research ratings and research that benefits the national economy and society at the nation-state level.

There are global problems such as pandemics, climate change, poverty, international wars and conflict, environ-mental pollution, malnourishment and hunger, global inequalities, lack of education, lack of security and well-being, and violence whose understanding and solution requires transnational research cooperation. Although transnational research funding is much needed, the reality is that nationalist research funding policies are dominant. Tackling global problems requires international, inter- and trans-disciplinary cooperation in research. There already is a significant level of such cooperation but a lack of transnational funding schemes.

Neo-colonialism does not merely mean imperialist forms of culture. Political Economy plays a major role. It is therefore not enough that critical knowledge from scholars in the Global South is produced and acknowledged. De-colonisation needs to challenge the unequal political economy that under-pins knowledge production in global capitalism. This means, for example, that in the context of media and communication, we should be critical of, challenge and establish alternatives to a variety of aspects of neo-colonialism that will now be discussed.

4.2 Capitalist Academic Publishing

Many academic publishers are capitalist organisations making profit from publishing by selling books, article processing charges (APCs), access to databases and electronic learning, and research resources. Rich universities such as Oxford, Cambridge, Harvard, Yale, Stanford, MIT, etc. provide access to vast amounts of knowledge to their scholars and students, while the world's poor universities struggle to provide such access, which is a consequence of the capitalist organisation of academic knowledge production and distribution. Among the world's 50 richest universities, there are 41 US universities and no African and Latin American universities.[3] The world's largest and most prestigious academic publishers are based in the West. Inequalities in the access to knowledge are the result of the unequal global distribution of wealth in capitalist societies. Having access to the world's knowledge is an important aspect of producing new knowledge.

4.3 Academic Inequalities in Rankings and Metrics

In a world shaped by neoliberalism, academia has more and more become shaped by the quantification and metrification of knowledge and reputation. The logic of capitalist accumulation has more and more shaped the academic world in distinct forms, which has advanced the instrumental and reified character of the academic system.

---

3 Data source: https://www.nonprofitcollegesonline.com/wealthiest-universities-in-the-world/, accessed on 14 July 2021.

> Universities '*today are large systems of authoritative control, standardization, gradation, accountancy, classification, credits and penalties. We need to decolonize the systems of access and management insofar as they have turned higher education into a marketable product, rated, bought and sold by standard units, measured, counted and reduced to staple equivalence by impersonal, mechanical tests and therefore readily subject to statistical consistency, with numerical standards and units. We have to decolonize this because it is deterring students and teachers from a free pursuit of knowledge. It is substituting this goal of free pursuit of knowledge for another, the pursuit of credits. It is replacing scientific capacity and addiction to study and inquiry by salesman-like proficiency. [...] Then there is the mania for assessment. The system of business principles and statistical accountancy has resulted in an obsessive concern with the periodic and quantitative assessment of every facet of university functioning*'.
>
> (Mbeme 2016, 30–31)

It is no surprise that in the top-100 of university rankings such as the QS World University Ranking 2022, there are 30 North American universities (US and Canada), 34 European universities (including the UK), and no university from a country with medium or low human development (based on the UN Human Development Index).[4] In the QS World University Ranking 2022, the best ranked university from a

4 Data sources: https://www.topuniversities.com/university-rankings/world-university-rankings/2022, accessed on 14 July 2021, & United Nations (2020).

country that has medium or low human development was placed on position 177. The Indian Institute of Technology Bombay (#177), the Indian Institute of Technology Delhi (#185), and the Indian Institute of Science (#186) are the only universities from medium or low development countries ranked among the top 200 in the QS World University Ranking 2022.[5]

Global inequality also shapes journal rankings such as Web of Science (see Table 4.2). Among the 25 most-cited organisations in Web of Science, there are 18 US institutions and no universities located in countries with medium or low human development. Among the top 200 most-cited organisations, there is just one institution located in a country with medium or low human development, the Indian Institute of Technology System (rank 176).[6]

There is a connection between poverty, underdevelopment and the positions in academic rankings.

4.4 Unequal Reputation and Opportunities

The metrification of academia has consequences for the lives of academics. Those studying and working in high-reputation, rich universities have excellent chances to find highly paid, high-reputation jobs in industry, public services and academia; to obtain high, reputable research grants; to be published in the highest-ranking journals and by high-reputation publishers; to be recognised and listened to as important and influential voices in the academic field, the public sphere, the economy, polity and society.

---

5 Data source: https://www.topuniversities.com/university-rankings/world-university-rankings/2022, accessed on 14 July 2021.

6 Data source: https://incites.clarivate.com, accessed on 14 July 2021.

Table 4.2. Research Organisations Most Cited in Web of Science, 1980–14 July 2021.

Rank	Organisation	Country	Number of Citations
1	University of California System	US	57,302,843
2	Harvard	US	34,659,926
3	CNRS	France	25,630,904
4	University of London	US	21,190,225
5	National Institutes of Health	US	20,398,303
6	University of Texas	US	19,613,964
7	United States Department of Energy	US	17,933,111
8	Chinese Academy of Sciences	China	15,748,097
9	Pennsylvania Commonwealth System of Higher Education	US	14,798,371
10	Stanford University	US	14,235,746
11	Max Planck Society	Germany	14,056,600
12	Johns Hopkins University	US	12,721,453
13	University of Washington	US	12,418,892
14	University of Washington Seattle	US	12,313,084
15	University of Toronto	Canada	12,292,248
16	MIT	US	12,224,840
17	University of California Los Angeles	US	12,187,167
18	University of California Berkeley	US	11,904,456
19	University of Michigan System	US	11,588,868
20	University of Michigan	US	11,583,419
21	University of Oxford	UK	11,166,129
22	University College London	UK	10,764,204
23	University of Pennsylvania	US	10,648,978
24	Helmholtz Association	Germany	10,614,381
25	University of North Carolina	US	10,611,092

Source: https://incites.clarivate.com, accessed on 14 July 2021.

4.5 Wealth Inequalities in Academia

Rich universities have the material funds by which they can pay high salaries to their employees, provide high levels of university-funded research time and attract highly skilled researchers; they can invest in the development of highly skilled and high-impact research teams; can support academics with a high number of administrative support staff and research assistants; can provide high individual levels of financial support for travels to and attendance of academic conferences, networking events, policy events and industry events; can provide high investments for fieldwork, technologies, laboratories, libraries and other academic resources and can provide regular sabbaticals that increase the organisational and individual research performance, etc. In contrast, poor universities do not have the financial means to compete with the high investments made by and material support provided by rich universities. Such material inequalities translate into inequalities of research performance, reputation, visibility and influence in academia.

4.6 Class and Higher Education

In capitalist societies, higher education and academia are class structured. Children from rich and well-situated families tend to have much better chances, preconditions and financial possibilities to attend university in general and high-reputation universities in particular. The world's top-ranking universities have high tuition fees. Tuition fees as the commodification of higher education are an aspect of neo-colonial academia. Rich families can afford to pay these high fees as investment into the future of their children. Children from poor families and families that cannot afford such fees have to either take out student loans, which implies a life in debt, or compete for a limited number of scholarships. In addition, children from rich families often attend private elite schools because their parents can afford school fees, which gives advantages to such pupils when applying to university.

Elite universities are self-perpetuating systems, where academics coming predominantly from privileged backgrounds create future elites that take on leadership positions and positions of influence in the university system, the management and boards of transnational corporations, governments, public services, professions and public sphere organisations such as news media, lobbying groups, civil society organisations and think tanks. Members of working-class families – that is, families that are not rich and whose members work for wages, are freelancers, contributing family workers or members of the subproletariat that is unemployed and lives in absolute poverty – are largely excluded from the self-perpetuating system of elite academia.

Wealth and poverty influence higher education attainment. Tables 4.3 and 4.4 show data for higher education attainment among young people who finished secondary education in the five years before data collection. Higher education enrolment is high in rich countries and very low in the least developed countries, especially countries in Sub-Saharan Africa (see Table 4.3).

Young people from the poorest families are much more unlikely to attend university than those from the richest families (see Table 4.4). This gap exists both in rich and poor countries. There are indications that in poor countries, the gap between young people from rich and poor families who attend university is significantly larger than in more developed countries (see Table 4.4).

Table 4.3. Gross Attendance Rate for Tertiary Education, Year 2019 (or Latest Year Available), the Basic Population the Data Refer to is the 5-Year Age Group Immediately Following Upper Secondary Education.

Country	Share
World	38.8%
High-income countries	75.7%
Least developed countries	11.2%
Sub-Saharan Africa	9.2%
Europe	73.3%
Northern America	86.6%
Niger (lowest human Development Index in 2020, HDI rank 189)	4.2%
Central African Republic (HDI rank 188)	
Chad (HDI Rank 187)	3.3%
Burundi (HDI rank 185)	4.1%
Norway (highest human development, HDI rank 1)	83.0%
Ireland (HDI rank 2)	77.3%
Switzerland (HDI rank 3)	61.4%
UK (HDI rank 13)	61.4%
US (HDI rank 17)	88.3%

Source: UNESCO Institute for Statistics, accessed on 15 July 2021.

Completion of a higher education programme is in general higher among those who come from rich families than those who come from poor families (see Table 4.5). In the world's poorest countries, this gap is extreme: only those from the richest families have a chance to complete a university degree,

Table 4.4. Gross Attendance Rate for Tertiary Education, by Wealth Quintiles, Year 2019 (or Latest Year Available), the Basic Population the Data Refer to is the 5-Year Age Group Immediately Following Upper Secondary Education.

Country	Poorest Quintile	2nd Q	3rd Q	4th Q	Richest Quintile	Multiplication Factor Richest by Poorest Quintile
Chad (HDI rank 187, low human development)	0.2%	N/A	N/A	N/A	8.8%	44.0
Mali (HDI rank 184, low)	0.4%	0.7%	0.5%	4.0%	14.4%	36.0
Malawi (HDI rank 174, low)	0.2%	0.1%	0.4%	0.4%	10.0%	50.0
Senegal (HDI rank 168, low)	0.7%	2.3%	4.4%	5.5%	18.7%	26.7
Nigeria (HDI rank 161)	0.8%	3.1%	6.2%	13.9%	37.2%	46.5
Rwanda (HDI rank 160, low)	0.1%	N/A	0.6%	1.6%	12.5%	125.0
Georgia (HDI rank 61, very high development)	7.9%	23.5%	39.7%	57.8%	77.4%	9.8
Serbia (HDI rank 64, very high development)	35.3%	45.2%	73.8%	63.3%	89.7%	2.5
Albania (HDI rank 69, high development)	15.7%	29.7%	35.9%	52.1%	69.9%	4.5

Source: UNESCO Institute for Statistics, accessed on 15 July 2021.

whereas those in families belonging to other income groups are largely excluded from higher education (see Table 4.5).

Wealth and income are not the same as class status in a Marxian understanding of class. They are more in line with a

Table 4.5. Percentage of People Aged 25–29 Who Have Completed at Least Four Years of Higher Education, Latest Available Data.

Country	Poorest Quintile	2nd Q	3rd Q	4th Q	Richest Quintile
Low-income countries	6%	5%	5%	6%	17%
Canada (Human Development Index rank 16)	21%	24%	33%	44%	45%
Australia (HDI rank 8)	37%	44%	42%	54%	63%
Republic of Korea (HDI rank 23)	55%	57%	63%	68%	83%
Israel (HDI rank 19)	22%	39%	42%	43%	59%
Serbia (HDI rank 64)	18%	24%	27%	51%	61%
US (HDI rank 17)	22%	30%	44%	60%	71%
China (HDI rank 85)	15%	14%	16%	20%	35%
Uganda (HDI rank 159)	0%	0%	0%	0%	2%
Rwanda (HDI rank 160)	0%	0%	1%	8%	11%
Malawi (HDI rank 174)	0%	0%	N/A	N/A	6%
Sierra Leone (HDI rank 182)	0%	0%	0%	1%	4%
Mali (HDI rank 184)	0%	1%	1%	1%	8%
Burundi (HDI rank 185)	0%	0%	0%	0%	4%
Chad (HDI rank 187)	0%	0%	0%	0%	3%
Niger (HDI rank 189)	0%	0%	0%	0%	2%

Source: https://www.education-inequalities.org/, accessed on 16 July 2021.

Weberian definition of class that focuses on differences in life chances. In Marxian class analysis, the position in the production process and the (non-)control of the means of production and capital determines class status. Official socio-economic statistics tend to be based on a Weberian understanding of class. These statistics provide an approximation of data for Marxian analysis. The family of a CEO of a large company who has high income and owns parts of the company is very likely to be part of the richest wealth quintile. In Marxian terms, the CEO is part of the capitalist class. In contrast, the family of a wage-earning toilet cleaner is very likely to be part of one of the lowest wealth quintiles. The toilet cleaner is part of the working class in Marxian theory. The presented data indicate that class, wealth and poverty are important factors influencing access to and attainment of higher education.

Table 4.6 shows the results of an analysis of the class inequality of undergraduate admission to British universities. It was published by the Higher Education Policy Institute. The author of the policy paper for each university calculated a Gini coefficient based on the local areas where admitted undergraduate students live and a classification of the participation rates in higher education of these areas. Areas with a high participation rate are typically wards where well-off families live. Based on these data, one can identify the most equal and the most unequal British universities (Table 4.6). The most unequal universities tend to take in a high number of students from well-off local areas with high levels of participation in higher education and a low number of poorer local areas with low levels of participation. Seven of the 10 most unequal universities are Russell Group universities, a group of high prestige and very rich British universities.

Table 4.6. Socio-Economic (In)Equality in the Admission of Undergraduate Students in the UK

Rank (Highest Equality)	University	Rank (Highest Inequality)	University	
1	U of Hull	1	U of Cambridge	Russell Group
2	U of Derby	2	U of St Andrews	
3	Edge Hill U	3	U of Bristol	Russell Group
4	U of Chester	4	U of Oxford	Russell Group
5	Plymouth College of Art	5	U of Aberdeen	
6	York St John U	6	U of Edinburgh	Russell Group
7	Leeds Beckett U	7	UCL	Russell Group
8	U of Worcester	8	U of Durham	Russell Group
9	Anglia Ruskin U	9	Robert Gordon U	
10	Cardiff Metropolitan U	10	LSE	Russell Group

Source: Martin (2018).

In 2020, the 10 richest British universities measured in terms of their endowments were all members of the Russell Group.[7] Russell Group universities are universities that produce members of the future upper class and help reproduce the culture of this class by keeping out members of everyday families. Oxford and Cambridge are the two richest and most prestigious British universities. In 2015, 82% of the offers made at Oxford and 81% of offers made at Cambridge went to students from upper-class families (Weale, Adams and Bengtsson 2017). 'An average of 43% of offers from Oxford and 37% from Cambridge were made to privately educated students between 2010 and 2015, while just 7% of children overall are educated in private schools' (Weale, Adams and Bengtsson 2017). In 2020, the share of offers made to students at Oxford and Cambridge who attended private schools stood at 25.8% (Masters 2021), which means the class gap has been a bit reduced but still persists.

4.7 Management Hierarchies

The corporatisation, privatisation and commodification of universities have resulted in a weakening of democracy in many universities. Senior managers are mostly not elected by academic workers and student representatives, but appointed by small circles of other senior managers. They often act like CEOs who manage universities like capitalist businesses and bureaucratic organisations, which detaches decisions made at the top from the interests of academic workers.

7 https://en.wikipedia.org/wiki/University_of_Birmingham, accessed on 15 July 2021. https://en.wikipedia.org/wiki/Russell_Group, accessed on 15 July 2021.

4.8 The Capitalist University as Neo-Colonialism

Neo-colonialism has in academia meant the rise of the capitalist university and has brought about a variety of inequalities. The capitalist publishing system benefits the scholars from rich universities. The metrification of academic life reifies universities by focussing on quantity and accumulation instead of on academic qualities and sustains global academic inequalities, including unequal reputation and job and promotion opportunities. Rich universities dominate academia and play a key role in inequalities that shape the academic field at the global level. Those who come from poor families and working-class families are largely excluded from rich elite universities. Neo-colonialism commodifies access to universities in the form of tuition fees, which has perpetuated the exclusion of the poor and the working class. Under neo-colonial conditions, universities are often run like corporations and take on the role of creating instrumental knowledge and degrees that directly benefit capitalist interests and undermine the independence of universities and their capacities to advance critical analysis and critical reflection. The question arises if alternatives to academic capitalism and the neo-colonial character of universities are possible. The concluding section addresses this question.

5. CONCLUSION: FROM UNIVERSITY CAPITALISM TOWARDS THE PUBLIC INTEREST AND COMMONS-ORIENTED UNIVERSITY

Neo-colonialism has in neoliberal capitalism meant accumulation by dispossession, the commodification of (almost) everything, and the transnationalisation of capital in the form of global activities of transnational corporations.

Neo-colonialism has brought about what Boaventura de Sousa Santos (2018, 356) terms 'university capitalism', the university as a 'capitalist enterprise' and an organisation operating 'according to criteria proper to capitalism'. The university and especially elite universities have always had the role of helping to reproduce the ruling class and its economy, culture and politics in capitalist society. Increasingly, the realms of higher education and research have lost their relative independence and have become subsumed under the logic of capital and the commodity. The capitalist colonisation of academia has taken forms such as the creation and extension of for-profit academic publishing models, the metrification of academic reputation and knowledge; a highly unequal distribution of universities' wealth, resources, reputation and influence; the commodification of higher education in the form of tuition fees, the direct and indirect influence of corporations and capitalist logic on universities, agendas that reinforce the collaboration of universities with capitalist businesses and the creation of academic knowledge as an instrument of capitalist companies, the undemocratic management of universities as businesses, class inequalities in the access to universities and attainment of students and scholars in higher education. One of the important dimensions of the de-colonisation of the university is to drive back the logic of capitalism and to overcome class inequalities in academia and other inequalities that interact with class inequalities in academia.

The true de-colonisation of academia has to include weakening the logic of capitalism in this realm of society. The de-colonisation of academia includes the commonification, democratisation and self-management of academia. De-colonisation is not a moral question and not a question of individual behaviour, but first and foremost a question of political economy and power.

Commonification, democratisation and self-management as de-colonisation of the academic field means the creation of not-for-profit academic publishers; the abolishment of academic rankings, metrics and reputational hierarchies; the establishment of new transparent, inclusive, open and democratic forms of doing academia; publicly funded universities that throughout the world realise the human right to education, which includes the right of everyone to be able to afford and attend university and equitable access to higher education and requires proper taxation of capital and wealth in order to support the funding of higher education throughout the world; overcoming the gaps in wealth, reputation, influence and resources between rich and poor universities; the transformation of the neoliberal university into self-managed universities that are democratically managed by academic workers and students and that have no CEOs and executive boards; and the creation of a classless higher education, research and academic system where class status does not determine the chances of humans to enter and succeed in respectively to be excluded from and fail in academia.

Global capitalism shapes the situation of students, scholars and academic knowledge production in the Global South in manifold ways. The globalisation of capitalism and society has also resulted in a globalisation of higher education. More children from well-situated families in the Global South now attend Western universities and take on professional and academic jobs in the West. Globalisation has not meant the creation of general access to higher education and the resulting careers for children from poor families throughout the world. To de-colonise academia requires to globally challenge the gaps between the rich and the poor, capital and labour, the powerful and the powerless, and the dominant class and subordinated classes. It requires the de-commodification of higher education and to advance the logic of higher education, academia, knowledge and research as public goods and commons in societies worldwide.

Boaventura de Sousa Santos (2017, 2019) argues that the de-colonisation of the university is closely intertwined with de-commodification along the following dimensions: 'access to the university (for students) and access to a university career (for faculty); research and teaching contents; disciplines of knowledge, curricula, and syllabi; teaching/learning methods; institutional structure and university governance; and relations between the university and society at large' (Santos 2019, 221). We can summarise this distinction by saying that access, the production of content and knowledge, methods, governance and relations to society are key dimensions of academia and the university.

We will now along these dimensions present some recommendations and suggestions for university reforms that create material foundations for the de-colonisation of the university and academia. These are general suggestions transcending a particular field of study and research but as such also are highly relevant for the progressive and emancipatory transformation of Media and Communication Studies. These suggestions are a starting point and do not claim to be conclusive and complete.

5.1 Academia's Relations to Society

There should be proper taxation of transnational corporations, capital and billionaires. Global redistribution of this wealth would support proper public funding and public organisation of universities around the world. We need a public university instead of a capitalist university.

Parts of the endowed wealth of the world's richest universities should be socialised and globally redistributed in order to support poor universities and individuals from disadvantaged backgrounds.

Society should rethink and reposition the role of universities in society away from the corporate university that serves capitalist society towards the public interest and commons-oriented university that as public service advances critical knowledge, critical thinking, critical reading, critical writing, critical presenting, critical debate, critical making, critical creativity and critical cooperation. Critique is the essence of a progressive university. Critique is the opposite of instrumentalism. Knowledge is instrumental if it is an instrument of capitalism, governments or undemocratic forces. Critical knowledge challenges instrumentalism and stands in the interest of a good society that benefits all.

5.2 Access to the University and Academic Knowledge

There should be free access to higher education for everyone and more support of children from poor and working-class families in the form of scholarships and affirmative action that increase the share of students and faculty from lower socio-economic backgrounds and poor families.

There should be public funding, support and encouragement of not-for-profit (diamond) open-access journals and not-for-profit open-access book publishers as well as open access mandates for this type of open-access publishing. Diamond open access is the best way of advancing global access to academic knowledge for everyone (Fuchs and Sandoval 2013), which especially benefits poor universities and their scholars and students. For-profit open-access models that have high APCs in order to make profit are just like models where rich libraries pay high subscription fees, they are neo-colonial mechanisms that exclude the poor from access.

Metrification and 'evaluitis' in the academic system should be abolished and replaced by qualitative systems of knowledge search and metadata that encourage the encounter of and debate between humans and the engagement with their ideas. We need public funding for, support of, and the establishment of repositories and databases that include and index and do not quantify knowledge published in not-for-profit (diamond) open-access publications. Web of Science and similar metric systems characteristics for university capitalism should be replaced with such new diamond databases and repositories.

As long as metric systems such as Web of Science exist, there should be mandates that not-for-profit (diamond) open-access journals must be included.

5.3 The Production of Content and Knowledge

Universities need proper infrastructures and means of production. The general redistribution of wealth by taxing capital and the rich should benefit poor universities so that they can hire an adequate number of staff, increase staff salaries and create an adequate infrastructure (technology, quality of buildings, rooms and libraries, etc.).

There should be a weakening of research-funding nationalism, that is, the establishment of more national and international research funds that support international research cooperation so that partners from different countries, including from the Global South, can obtain funding that enables them to organise significant amounts of research time that allows proper investigation of key problems, conducting local and transnational research, and research cooperation.

English has become the academic lingua franca, which undoubtedly has to do with the US dominance of the world system since the Second World War and gives advantages in global academia to those whose native language is English. At the same time, if the world's academics were to only publish in their native languages, then isolated and fragmented national and regional academic systems of knowledge production would be the result. Not publishing in English is also no solution. What we need is academic publishing in multiple languages and proper public funding of academic translations. Not-for-profit academic publishers should receive special public funds for making and publishing translations. Making non-Western scholars globally visible is not simply a matter of morality, but also one of language, translation, availability, accessibility and funding of these processes.

At the level of academic content, there should be encouragement of the production and use of critical knowledge in research and the classroom that helps advance the public good and a good society for all, which includes knowledge that critically analyses exploitation and domination, fascism, war, imperialism, violence, genocide, capitalism, racism, nationalism, classism, gender-based oppression, etc.

5.4 Research Methods

All methods should be encouraged that help to shed light on and better understand exploitation and domination and that create knowledge that has the potential to support the advancement of the public good and a good society that benefits all. Methodology should not be the use of methods for the sake of methods but the use of whatever methods are needed for answering questions that are crucial for the critique of oppression and fostering a good society. Theory is in itself a methodology and helps us to come to terms with the world and discuss normative, moral and political questions and deal with the big questions of society and the world. Empirical research should be theory driven. Positivism detaches empirical research from theory or reduces theory to an instrument of empiricism. Positivism conducts empirical analysis in order to show how the world looks like without the critical imperative to create knowledge and interpretations of the world that inform changing the world. Research should be anti-positivist and combine theory, empirical research and philosophy/ethics. It should integrate the experiences and relate to struggles of the exploited and the oppressed. These groups are not 'stakeholders', a term that originated in capitalist businesses, but classes and subjects.

In the social sciences and humanities, including Media and Communication Studies and Internet Research, digital methods have been established as a new type of positivism, a digital positivism that uses big data analytics ('computational social science', 'digital humanities') for purely describing the world in quantitative terms (Fuchs 2017). We need critical theories combined with critical methods in order to critically understand and change the world, including digitalisation and its roles in society. Research should advance human interests and include the oppressed and their interests in the research process. Trans-disciplinarity should be supported and advanced in the form of critical research that studies all societal dimensions of phenomena and uses philosophy as a meta-scientific approach that allows us to ask and find answers to the big questions of the world.

5.5 Governance

The capitalist and corporate university should be transformed into the democratic, self-managed, transparent university that is run by academic workers and students and not by neoliberal managers and CEOs. Precarious, casual academic labour should be ended and academic workers' rights be strengthened. Teaching in universities should be organised in ways that advance students' critical thinking and action capacities. Such teaching is a pedagogy of empowerment and critical pedagogy (see Giroux 2020).

Neo-colonialism has established new forms of global exploitation, exclusion and domination where transnational capital, the logic of commodification and instrumental reason play a key role. University capitalism and the corporate, instrumental university have been the result of neo-colonialism. To de-colonise the university means to transform university capitalism into public-interest and commons-oriented universities that advance the public good and a good society. It means to challenge neo-colonialism.

5

ROBOTS AND ARTIFICIAL INTELLIGENCE (AI) IN DIGITAL CAPITALISM

1. INTRODUCTION

Robots and Artificial Intelligence (AI) have become part of the everyday life of many humans. They mow loans and vacuum floors. Robots operate as virtual assistants and smart speakers (Amazon Alexa, Amazon Echo, Siri, Google Assistant etc.) that provide information, play videos and music, read audiobooks, order goods online, or are customer service agents. Robots drive some vehicles such as trains and operate as assistant systems in cars that correct driver errors in order to avoid accidents, park cars, display driving information, or control the car's speed (cruise control). Surgeons are assisted by robotic systems. On the Internet, bots post and crawl information, gather data about users, provide customer information, or create and spread information and attention including fake news. Emergency robots help distinguish fires, search for victims after earthquakes and other disasters underground, in the air, underwater, or in rough terrains etc.

Drones are aerial robots that monitor the environment, conduct surveillance of humans and the environment, or shoot bombs from the air. A smart home is an AI-based robotic system that regulates the supply of energy, heat, water and the operation of household devices such as the refrigerator, the oven, the television, the stereo and other entertainment systems.

Robots are no longer just operating in manufacturing and sciences such as space exploration. They have entered culture at large. We can therefore ask: How can we understand and theorise the impacts of robots and AI on everyday life based on Radical Humanism? How can Lefebvre's ideas be used to reveal the ideological character of contemporary accounts of the impacts of robots and AI on society?

In this essay, we utilise the French critical theorist Henri Lefebvre's works for giving answers to this question. Lefebvre is well known for his three volume *Critique of Everyday Life* as well as his sociology of space in *The Production of Space*. It is hardly known that he also wrote a book about robotics and cybernetics. The reason is that *Vers le cybernanthrope* (*Towards the Cybernanthrope*, 1971) has thus far not been translated into English. With 98 citations, the book has been relatively little read and cited.[1] At the same time, the *Production of Space* had received 47,335 citations.[2] A book little read does not mean it is unimportant. In the case of Lefebvre's book on the cybernanthrope, there is a variety of reasons, including the lack of an English translation. In this chapter, I

1 https://scholar.google.com/scholar?cites=13517513437426862518&as_sdt=2005&sciodt=0,5&hl=en, accessed on 19 June 2021.

2 https://scholar.google.com/scholar?hl=en&as_sdt=0%2C5&q=Lefebvre+production+of+space+&btnG=

read Lefebvre's writings on cybernetics and robotics in the light of contemporary debates and developments.

Lefebvre was a Radical Humanist. Erich Fromm defines Radical Humanism as 'a global philosophy which emphasizes the oneness of the human race, the capacity of man to develop his own powers and to arrive at inner harmony and at the establishment of a peaceful world' (Fromm 1966, 14–15).

Section 2 introduces Lefebvre's notion of the cybernanthrope and sets it in relation to robots and AI in contemporary society. Based on Lefebvre's critique of the cybernanthrope, Section 3 develops foundations of the ideology critique of robots and AI in digital capitalism. The section discusses examples of technological deterministic and social constructivist thought in the context of robotics, AI and cyborgs. It argues for a Lefebvrian, dialectical, Radical Humanist approach. Based on Lefebvre, Section 4 situates Radical Humanism in the context of computing, AI and robotics.

2. THE CYBERNANTHROPE

The French word for 'cybernetics' is « cybernétique ». The word phrase « anthrope » as in the French words « anthropologie » (anthropology) and « anthropique » (anthropogenic) is a reference to the human. The word 'cybernantrhope' that Lefebvre created therefore points towards the combination of computers and humans and the transformation of human beings by computers and robots. The cybernanthrope is a 'strange couple' (2016, 164) of computer and human. 'The two entities, automaton and human, meet up in a single category: the Cybernanthrope!' (Lefebvre 2016, 181).

The reader will be reminded of the notion of the cyborg that comes from science fiction literature and movies. The term was introduced in 1960 by Manfred E. Clynes and

Nathan S. Kline (1960/1995) for describing technological enhancements of the human body that allows humans to survive in outer space. Cyborgs are 'self-regulating man-machine systems' that deliberately incorporate 'exogenous components extending the self-regulatory control function of the organism in order to adapt it to new environments' (Clynes and Kline 1960/1995, 29–30).

The most cited academic work on cyborgs is Donna Haraway's (1991, 149–181) *A Cyborg Manifesto* that was first published in 1985. For Haraway, the 'cyborg is a cybernetic organism, a hybrid of machine and organism, a creature of social reality as well as a creature of fiction' (Haraway 1991, 149). Lefebvre's cybernanthrope is not the same as the cyborg. Whereas the cyborg is a hybrid being, more machine than human, the cybernanthrope means the ideology of technocracy and the ideologues associated with the existence of the cyborg, computers and robots in society. The cybernanthrope is 'a technological and rational attitude. [...] It is fascinating to compare this with Haraway's cyborg. [...] Lefebvre identifies what one risks losing if one treats oneself, and by implication, others, as machines' (Shields 1999, 74, 101, 102). 'For Lefebvre, the cybernanthrope was the antihumanist incarnate, a reviled man cum machine, the air-conditioned official obsessed with information systems, with scientific rationality, with classification and control' (Merrifield 2006, 89).

The cybernanthrope has resulted in the creation of robots (Lefebvre 1971b, 193). According to Lefebvre, the robot is often ideologically imagined as being perfect and acting perfectly. 'The cybernanthrope deplores human weakness and weaknesses. They know their imperfections. The human, the human quality, they disavow them. They disqualify Humanism, in thought and in action. They hunt down the illusions of subjectivity: creation, happiness, passion, as empty as oblivion' (1971b, 194).[3] The cybernanthrope believes in the perfectness of the robot and computers and that these machines have to bring about a better society. The cybernanthrope wants to destroy spontaneity, imagination, fantasy and poetry (1971b, 194). According to Lefebvre, the cybernanthrope and robotics are about precise definitions and measurements, 'quantifiable qualities'. What suits the cybernanthrope is defined functionally and structurally. The cybernanthrope is averse to unknown, too rich, too surprising flavours (1971b, 198).[4] The cybernanthrope creates superspectacles, the 'total spectacle' that 'makes spectacles of itself and sells spectacles' (1971b, 201–202).[5] The cybernanthrope as the subjectivity and impersonation of the ideology of automation permeates society: 'We only know that there are cybernanthropes wherever there are models, patterns, stereotypes, prototypes, genotypes, statuses, roles, mimesis, functions, structures, in other words, everywhere' (1971b, 204).[6]

Whereas Haraway's cyborg has a rather neutral category that describes human/machine hybrids and can both be

3 Translated from French: « Le cybernanthrope déplore la faiblesse humaine et ses faiblesses. Il connait ses imperfections. L'humain, la qualité humaine, il les désavoue. Il disqualifie l'humanisme, en pensée et en action. Les illusions de la subjectivité, il les pourchasse: la création, le bonheur, la passion, aussi vides que l'oubli. »

4 Translated from French: « des qualités quantifiables. Ce qui convient au cybernanthrope se définit fonctionnellement et structuralement. Le cybernanthrop se défie des saveurs inconnues, trop riches, trop surprenantes. »

5 Translated from French: « le Spectacle total», « qui se donne en spectacle et vend du spectacle ».

6 Translated from French: « Nous savons seulement qu'il y a cybernanthropes partout où il y a modèles, < patterns >, stéréotypes, prototypes, génotypes, statuts, rôles, mimésis, fonctions, structures, c'est-à-dire partout. »

utilised by forms of domination (the informatics of domination) and emancipation, the cybernanthrope has an ideological character. Whereas Haraway's cyborg is Posthumanist, Lefebvre's cybernanthrope is anti-Humanist. Whereas Haraway is a post-structuralist, Lefebvre is a Marxist Humanist. Whereas Haraway sees Humanism as inherently dualist and repressive, Lefebvre distinguishes between the essence of human beings and the reality of Liberal Humanism as ideology. While Haraway rejects and opposes Marxist Humanism, Lefebvre sees Radical, Marxist and Socialist Humanism as the project that defends humans and society against totalitarian political economy.

The robot is a machine and therefore not human. The cyborg is a robot that according to its proponents incorporates and duplicates human qualities. It is not human, but transcends humans. It is Transhuman and Post-human. We have already seen definitions of the cyborg. But what is a robot?

Based on the International Standard of Organisation (ISO), Saha (2014, 2) defines a robot as 'a *reprogrammable, multi-functional* manipulator designed to move material, parts, tools or specialized devices through variable programmed motions for the performance of a variety of tasks'. Winfield (2012, Table 1) argues that all robots have aspects of sensing, signalling, moving, changing their outside world, energy and a body. For him, robots feature '1. an artificial device that can *sense* its environment and *purposefully act* on or in that environment; 2. an *embodied* artificial intelligence; or 3. a machine that can *autonomously* carry out useful work' (Winfield 2012, 8).

Robots are computers that are based on software programmes, programmed code and algorithms that perceive their environment as well as act, interact and bring about changes in this environment.

Artificial Intelligence systems are technologies that simulate human intelligence, including learning, perception, or problem-solving. AI systems are 'machines that behave as though they were intelligent' (Ertel 2017, 1). 'Artificial intelligence (AI) seeks to make computers do the sorts of things that minds can do' (Boden 2018, 1). Not all robots are AI systems and not all AI systems are robots. But there is an intersection of the two technologies, AI robots are 'mechanical creatures which can function autonomously. "Intelligent" implies that the robot does not do things in a mindless, repetitive way; it is the opposite of the connotation from factory automation. [...] "Function autonomously" indicates that the robot can operate, self-contained, under all reasonable conditions without requiring recourse to a human operator. Autonomy means that a robot can adapt to changes in its environment (the lights get turned off) or itself (a part breaks) and continue to reach its goal' (Murphy 2000, 3–4).

There have been attempts to classify robots, but most of them are not grounded in theory and do not define a criterion of distinction, which makes them arbitrary, incomplete, unsystematic or overlapping. Saha (2014, 4) distinguishes between industrial and non-industrial/special-purpose robots. He identifies the following application areas of robots: medical robots, mining robots, space robots, underwater robots, defence robots, security robots, domestic robots, entertainment robots (Saha 2014, 8–12). All on Robots (2021) and Intro-Books (2018, chapter 4) identify different types of robots based on application areas: industrial robots, domestic or household robots, medical robots, service robots, military robots, entertainment robots, space robots, hobby and competition robots. Thomas (2019) mentions the following realms of society as the ones where AI and robotics have the highest impact: transportation, manufacturing, healthcare, education, media and customer service. Trovato et al. (2021) argue that humans feature perception, intentions and emotions; animals only perception; and robots none of these three features. Robots are bodies without a soul. The authors distinguish between anthropomorphic robots (robots modelled on humans), zoomorphic robots (robots modelled on animals), idiomorphic robots (robots that are objects shaped according to the functions they fulfil), physimorphic robots (robots modelled on something natural) and theomorphic robots (robots modelled on the divine and supernatural). This taxonomy of robots derives from the division of the world into humans, animals, nature, objects and the divine.

A more systematic typology of robots can be constructed by the focus on the realms of society where they act. In order to do so, one requires a model of society. Society is a spatio-temporally relatively consistent totality of human practices that produces and reproduces social relations and structures that enable and constrain further practices that are organised within the economic, the political and the cultural realms of society (Fuchs 2008, 2020a). The economic system of production is foundational in that production is an economic process (Fuchs 2020a). It is the system where humans produce goods and services in order to satisfy their needs. But the economic is preserved in, transformed by and sublated into other realms of society, namely the political and the cultural realms. Politics is the realm of society where humans produce and enforce collectively binding decisions for all members of society. Culture is the realm of society where humans produce meanings and definitions of the world and reproduce their bodies and their minds.

Robots can act in society's economic, political or cultural realm as well as in several different realms and social systems at the same time. For constructing a typology, besides the realm(s) where robots are applied, we need a second dimension of distinction. The chosen criterion relates to one of the most widely discussed questions about robots, namely the question if robots can, will and should replace humans.

John Searle (1990) distinguishes between strong AI and weak AI. Strong AI assumes that computers can duplicate the human mind, that computers can be made to think and that programmes are constitutive of thinking. 'Strong AI claims that thinking is merely the manipulation of formal symbols, and that is exactly what the computer does manipulate formal symbols. Its view is often summarized by saying, "The mind is to the brain as the program is to the hardware"' (Searle 1990, 26). In contrast, weak AI argues that computers can merely simulate human thought and are not equivalent to humans:

> *Just manipulating the symbols is not by itself enough to guarantee cognition, perception, understanding, thinking and so forth. And since computers, qua computers, are symbol-manip ulating devices, merely running the computer program is not enough to guarantee cognition. [...] As far as simulation is concerned, there is no difficulty in programming my computer so that it prints out, 'I love you, Suzy'; 'Ha ha'; or 'I am suffering the angst of postindustrial society under late capitalism'. The important point is that simulation is not the same as duplication, and that fact holds as much import for thinking about arithmetic as it does for feeling angst.*
>
> (Searle 1990, 26, 31)

Generalising Searle's distinction, we can define strong robotics as the claim that humans can fully duplicate humans and can therefore replace their activities and thought. Weak robotics argues that robots are not humans and therefore can never fully replace human activities and cannot think and feel. There are therefore limits to what human activities robots can replace. Complex forms of humans' work that involve affectual work, empathy and morality cannot be replaced by robots. If such a replacement is tried, then there is a high risk that there will be negative impacts on society.

Table 5.1 shows a typology of robots that uses the three realms of society as one dimension and the distinction between strong and weak robotics (substitution VS. simulation) as the other one. It also lists some examples for each type of robot. The typology identifies six types of robots.

Having established what robots and AI are, we will in the next section take a Lefebvrian approach to the analysis of ideology in the context of robots and AI:

3. ROBOTS, AI AND IDEOLOGY IN DIGITAL CAPITALISM

This section first outlines three approaches to the study of technology and society (3.1). It then advances an ideology critique of two of these approaches, namely technological determinism (3.2) and the social construction of technology (3.3) in the context of robots and AI that is based on the third approach, namely dialectics.

3.1 Three Approaches to the Analysis of Technology, Robots and AI

For Lefebvre, the world is dialectical. It is full of contradictions. Trying to make the world calculable and operating as if it were perfectly calculable, as computers and robots do, is a reduction of the world and the dialectic to dualism, the logic of strict separation.

Computing and robotics are undialectical. Computers process reality in terms of either/or, if then else, zeros and

Table 5.1. A Typology of Robots.

	Economy	Politics	Culture
Substitution of human activity	*Robot workers that replace human workers:* e.g. self-driving cars, robot vacuum cleaner, robot lawn mower, advertising and marketing bots, vending machines, self-service checkout, robotic packaging and delivery, manufacturing robots, personal digital assistants, agricultural robots, customer service robots, robot servants	*Robotic decision-making, administration and violence*: e.g. surveillance drones, military drones, robot soldiers, facial recognition CCTV, automated passport gates, robot judges, automated decision-making, virtual/AI politicians, robocops, robotic citizens, robotic prison guards, political bots on the Internet,	*Robotic minds:* e.g. robotic sex partners, robot psychotherapy [robotherapy], chess and game robots, (physical and emotional) care robots, automated/robot journalism, virtual celebrities/musicians/influencers/actors/artists, robotic art, robot teachers, automated translation, emotional robots, robot scientists (e.g. robonauts), automated science, fake news bots, deepfake video and audio
Augmentation of human activity	*Robot workers that support human work:* e.g. robot-assisted surgery, robot-assisted diagnosis, autopilot in vehicles, parking assist systems, medical and industrial exoskeletons/robot suits, robotic prostheses that support human activity	*Robot-assisted decision making, administration and violence:* document classification, handling and verification in public administration, support of crime reporting, support of the processing of permit applications, military exoskeletons/robot suits	*Robot-assisted mental activities:* e.g. robot care assistants, AI-assisted journalism, robot-assisted teaching and instruction, predictive analytics, AI-assisted analysis

ones. There is no in-between and transcendental reality for computers. Lefebvre argues in this context:

> *The cybernanthrope can be seen in his way of* reducing *what they touch, and first of all of* reducing *the contradictions. They put the greatest tenacity into this. This is their method of thinking and acting. They do not believe in the fruitfulness of conflicts. They stubbornly refuse the 'three terms' (the work, the joy, the drama, the revolutionary creation) that could arise from contradictions. They have little, if any, confidence in the sublation. They refuse any other possibility than their own confirmation and consolidation: their balance.*[7]
>
> (Lefebvre 1971b, 205)

Lefebvre writes that in contemporary society, the syntactic dimension of language is privileged, which becomes evident in 'technicity, machines, cybernetics, information theory. With the ideology that goes with it: the cult of technology, operationalism, the effective (practical) reduction of the human being to the dimension that can be best handled technically' (Lefebvre 1966, 282).[8]

---

7 Translated from French: « Le cybernanthrope se décèle à sa manière de *réduire* ce qu'il touche et d'abord de *réduire* les contradictions. Il y met la plus grande ténacité. C'est sa méthode de pensée et d'action. Il ne croit absolument pas en la fécondité des conflits. Il refuse obstinément les < troisiémes termes > (l'oeuvre, la joie, le drame, la création révolutionnaire) qui pourraient naitre des contradictions. Il a peu de confiance, pour ne pas dire aucune, dans le dépassement. Il refuse toute autre possibilité que sa propre confirmation et sa consolidation: son équilibre. »

8 Translated from French: « la technicité, les machines, la cybernétique, la théorie de l'informa tion. Avec l'idéologie qui s'y joint: culte de la technique, opérationalisme, réduction effective (pratique) de l'être humain à la dimension la mieux manipu lable techniquement. »

Lefebvre argues that the cybernanthropes want to make themselves global and planetary. Cybernanthroposes can be challenged by the irreducible (Lefebvre 1971b, 209). Irony, humour, the comical, satire, passion, disorder, desires are among the spiritual weapons of the anti-cybernanthropes (Lefebvre 1971b, 211–213).

The technocratic ideology characteristic of cybernanthropes is for Lefebvre a form of structuralism. He was a major critic of structuralism and its representatives (see Lefebvre 1971a). Structuralism is an ideology that links structural linguistics, information and communications theory, and perception theory (Lefebvre 2016, 172). It does not proceed 'according to poiesis, continuing physis, but according to mimesis' (2016, 173).

Structuralism is a reductionism that brackets out the 'concrete complexity of praxis, that of man and that of the world. Dialectics. Tragedy. Emotion and passion. The individual, certainly and perhaps a large part of the social. And then history' (2016, 176, see also 202). Structuralism is dualist: it 'separates, divides, classifies (into genres and kinds), determines formal differences, paradigms, conjunctions and disjunctions, binary oppositions, questions that it answers by a "yes" or a "no"' (2016, 176).

Lefebvre argues that Leibniz was a precursor to binary logic. 'But instead of the progression of tens, I have for many years used the simplest progression of all, which proceeds by twos, having found that it is useful for the perfection of the science of numbers. Thus I use no other characters in it bar 0 and 1, and when reaching two, I start again' (Leibniz, 1703). Gottfried Wilhelm Leibniz introduced the binary arithmetic that the logic of computing is built upon. Binary number systems had already before Leibniz played a role in China, Egypt, India and other cultures. In the middle of the nineteenth-century, George Boole further developed the binary number system into Boolean algebra. Claude E. Shannon showed in the late 1930s that relays can be used for building hardware that operates based on Boolean algebra. Around the same time, Alan Turing developed the notion of the Turing machine, which is the concept of the computer, and built one of the first computers. Soon thereafter, the first relay and vacuum tube computers were built that were in the 1940s replaced by transistor computers made of semiconductors ('second generation computing') that in turn were replaced by integrated circuits ('third generation computing') and microprocessors ('fourth generation computing').

By being based on reductionism and neglecting dialectics, traditional philosophy, cybernetics, information theory, linguistics, structuralism etc., created residues that are unaccounted for (Lefebvre 2016). For Lefebvre (2016), the task of metaphilosophy is to dialectically integrate residues into the analysis, which is a creative act of poiesis. This means that for Lefebvre, metaphilosophy incorporates the non-philosophical, praxis, freedom, desire, the human being, totality etc., into philosophy.

Computing is not problematic as such. Designed in the right manner and used in the right ways, computers are powerful tools for helping to advance societies where all humans benefit. Computers are media and tools, not causes. The problem is the uncritical approach to computing that reduces society to computing and sees the computer as the determining factor of society's development. Digital determinism is a form of technological determinism that argues that the computer is the one cause of certain phenomena in society. This logic is one-dimensional because it sees technology as the cause and determining factor of society and disregards how society's contradictions shape its development.

Table 5.2 shows three approaches in the sociology and philosophy of technology that analyse the relationship

Table 5.2. Approaches to the Analysis of the Relationship Between Technology and Society.

	Positive Moral Assessment	Negative Moral Assessment
Technological determinism	Technological optimism	Technological pessimism
Social constructivism	Socio-optimism	Socio-pessimism
Dialectical logic	Dialectic of society and technology	

between technology and society. In respect to how one can conceive of the relationship between technology and society, there are three sociological approaches: technological determinism, social constructivism and dialectical logic. Technological determinism reduces the relationship between technology and society to technology; social construction of technology approaches reduce the relationship between technology and society to society. The first disregards society's dynamics, the second does not take into account that technology's uses and impacts cannot be fully planned and foreseen and that there are often unintended consequences of technology's use in society.

Dialectical approaches take Lefebvre's reminder seriously that there are contradictions in society and contradictions of technology in society. Technologies have multiple potentials and affordances. What impacts their use is not fully determined in advance, but depends on the shaping of technologies and the political, economic and cultural context of use. Technologies' usages often do not have one single effect, but multiple contradictory potentials and realities. The relationship between technologies and society is a realm of contradictions and in antagonistic societies an arena of class and social struggles.

One important aspect of Table 5.2 has to do with morality and ethics, namely the question of how one assesses certain techno-social phenomena. Primarily positive assessments of technology, its uses and impacts on society are termed 'technological optimism', negative ones 'technological pessimism'. Dialectical ethics stresses that technologies have multiple, often contradictory, potentials and that the decisive factor is that humans collectively struggle for advancing usages of technology that support equality, freedom, justice and solidarity (Fuchs 2021b).

Fig. 5.1 visualises the logic of technological determinism, social constructivism and dialectics.

3.2 Robots in the Economy and Society: A Critique of Technological Determinism

3.2.1. Technological Determinism in Post-Humanism and Transhumanism

Let us have a look at the logics of how to understand the relationship between technology and society and how these logics have shaped the discussion of the role of robots in society and the economy.

Donna Haraway, author of *A Cyborg Manifesto*, is a technological optimist. Her works on cyborgs are optimistic about the effects of the creation of cyborgs on society. In a nutshell, she says that a cyborg society will abolish patriarchy, racism and capitalism. Her optimism becomes evident in formulations such as the following ones: 'The cyborg is our ontology; it gives us our politics' (Haraway 1991, 150); 'cyborg politics insist on noise and advocate pollution, rejoicing in the illegitimate fusions of animal and machine' (Haraway 1991, 176). 'The cyborg is a creature in a post-gender world' (Haraway 1991, 150). The notion of 'cyborg politics' is a

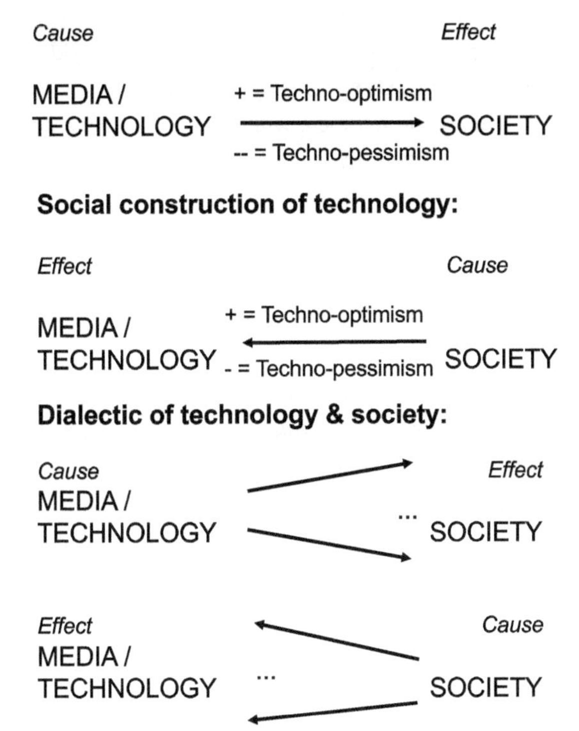

Fig. 5.1. Visualisation of Three Logics in the Study of Technology and Society.

technological determinist construct. It implies that there is a politics inherent in machines. Post-humanism displaces politics from the realm of social relations between humans into the world of machines.

Another example of techno-determinist techno-optimism can be found in the works of technological futurists such as Hans Moravec and Ray Kurzweil. They argue that robotics, nanotechnology and biotechnology will make humans immortal by turning into cyborgs. Moravec claims that 'we could "download" our minds directly into a body in the simulation. Alternatively, we could bring people out of the simulation by reversing the process – linking their minds to an outside robot body, or uploading them directly into it' (Moravec 1988, 123–124). He argues that there will be robot surgeons who kill humans in the process of transforming them into immortal robots:

> *The robot surgeon opens your brain case and places a hand on the brain's surface. [...] Layer after layer the brain is simulated, then excavated. Eventually your skull is empty, and the surgeon's hand rests deep in your brainstem. Though you have not lost consciousness, or even your train of thought, your mind has been removed from the brain and transferred to a machine. In a final, disorienting step the surgeon lifts out his hand. Your suddenly abandoned body goes into spasms and dies.*
>
> (Moravec 1988, 109–110)

Kurzweil calls the fusion of robots and humans the Singularity. 'By the time of the Singularity, there won't be a distinction between humans and technology. *This is not because humans will have become what we think of as machines today, but rather machines will have progressed to be like humans and beyond*' (Kurzweil 2005, 69). He is optimistic that the brain scanning Moravec talks about will exist by the end of the 2020s:

> *To capture this level of detail will require scanning from within the brain using nanobots, the technology for which will be available by the late 2020s. Thus, the early 2030s is a reasonable time frame for the computational performance, memory, and brain-scanning prerequisites of uploading. Like any*

> *other technology, it will take some iterative refinement to perfect this capability, so the end of the 2030s is a conservative projection for successful uploading.*
>
> (Kurzweil 2005, 164)

Transhumanists such as Moravec and Kurzweil are classical technological determinists. They are fascinated by the rise of new technologies, especially robots, nanotechnologies, AI and genetic engineering. Their fascination results in the fetishism of these technologies. Their approaches are detached from questions of political economy and power. In a capitalist society, power, property and influence are asymmetrically distributed. There are dominant classes and groups who in cyborg capitalism would be able to shape the conditions under which brain scans and cyborg-creation take place. In a capitalist society, one can easily imagine that dominant classes and groups would try to and struggle for reserving immortality for themselves and keep the members of the working-class mortal in order to limit proletarian power. In cyberborg capitalism, they are furthermore likely to try to ideologically manipulate cyborgs' brain contents in order to make them docile and prevent the rise of alternatives to class society. Killing humans in the process of transforming them into robots is morally highly questionable. It violates the Hippocratic Oath. Once such a moral threshold has been passed, there is under capitalist conditions the danger that certain humans are killed and not transformed into cyborgs because of their worldviews, class, ethnicity, origin, gender, skin colour etc.

There are also techno-pessimistic, techno-determinist assessments of robots in society that assume that robotics has to inevitably lead to fascism. For example:

> *Transhumanism: We believe that, by using the new technologies, the concept of human dignity loses its*

> *value since the superiority of enhanced people contradicts the principle of equality. From our point of view, besides the above mentioned issues, the transhumanist project involves other aspects related to the desire to dominate: on the one hand, we are facing a new form of slavery in the context of a technologized society and, on the other hand, a new form of totalitarianism, without involving elements related to language discourse, political parties, etc. This is about trying to overpower the human race by using the new technologies or to dominate the future through the quantum global brain. [...] we believe the transhumanist project could bring major harm to the current human species, minimizing the importance of the human rights and the true values of the contemporary society: justice, freedom, equality [...] We believed it would be important to analyze the negative aspects of transhumanism since they involve, on the one hand, denying all human values – justice, freedom, equality – and, on the other hand, substituting the human species and therefore substituting divinity. In our opinion, we cannot be certain that robots could make the difference between good and evil and so much the less could have a quantum global brain; on the contrary, they might get us back to a new totalitarian era, a soft type of totalitarianism.*
>
> (Terec-Vlad & Terec-Vlad 2014, 72–74)

It is certainly important to warn about the fascist potentials of versions of Transhumanism and Posthumanism that have to do with these approaches' nihilistic rejection of and opposition to Humanism. But robotics, nanotechnologies and biotechnologies are not inherently and automatically capitalist, colonialist, imperialist, totalitarian, racist, fascist, sexist etc. There are political-economic and cultural-ideological contexts of technology development, design and use. And many technologies have unpredictable dynamics.

Robotics and other technologies are more likely to be put to fascist and other problematic uses under capitalist than under democratic-socialist conditions. But struggles for humane and democratic uses of technologies are also possible in and against capitalism. Also in a democratic-socialist society, technologies are not perfect, so there is always a risk that they have unintended negative consequences or that values characteristic of class and dominative societies are designed into these technologies or shape certain forms of use. The point of a dialectical understanding of robots and technologies in general is that praxis and social struggles are the decisive aspect of society and technologies' impacts on and roles in society.

One problem of of many Transhumanist and Post-humanist analyses of robots is that they tend to give a dualist answer to the mind/body-problem. Like many religions, they assume that the human soul can be disentangled from the human mind. Whereas many religions argue that after a human person's death their soul can live on or transmigrate; Post-humanists and Transhumanists in a comparable manner assume that the soul and mind can be detached from the human body and can transmigrate into a computer. They argue that the brain is a machine that can be treated and analysed like a computer programme. They assume that the mind can be reduced to bits and that it is thereby possible to detach its content from the human body. They believe that technological reduction enables a dualistic split of mind and body.

Dialectical approaches in contrast to Transhumanism and Post-humanism assume that there is a dialectic of the mind and the body that cannot be disentangled and that therefore the transmigration of the soul and the mind is not possible. It is a form of philosophical idealism to assume that cyborgs which replace humans can be created.

One should, however, not as such rule out the possibility and desirability of the use of robots, nanotechnologies and biotechnologies for enhancing the quality of life and good lifetime of humans. It is practical socialism to improve the lives and living conditions of all humans. Robotic limbs can enhance the living quality of humans who are missing one or more limbs. Nanobots that detect illnesses in the human body and reinvigorate the body in order to increase humans' lifetime should be welcome. The point is that humans cannot and should not be replaced by machines, but that machines should be designed and put to use in manners that improve the lives of all humans. Socialist tech-politics, for example must include the availability of life-enhancing technologies not just for the privileged few but all humans, which requires us to think about the public funding of the healthcare system, the harms caused by the latter's privatisation and commodification, etc.

3.2.2. The Wired Brain as Post-Humanist and Transhumanist Ideology

Slavoj Žižek argues that contemporary visions of the Internet of Things, cyborgs, genetic engineering, AI and the wired brain, and digital automation show 'an attempt to integrate the passage to post-humanity into capitalism' (Žižek 2021, 41, see also Žižek 2020, Žižek 2018, chapter 1, Žižek 2017, chapter 4, Žižek 2016, chapter 1). In Post-humanism and Transhumanism, 'emancipation of humanity turns into emancipation from humanity' (Žižek 2016, 29). Žižek writes that the danger is that in the future, 'some will still have freedom, while others will be totally regulated by digital machinery' (Žižek 2017, 134) so that some will become new digital superhumans controlling power and the others will form a lower class or caste of unfree humans. Post-humanist developments undermine 'the very core of what it means to be a human being' (Žižek 2016, 29).

For Žižek (2020), a wired brain is a system that connects human brains to digital machines so that humans can change the status of digital machines with their thoughts and their brains can be read, manipulated, controlled and connected via digital machines. Such a system requires the implantation of neurotechnologies into human brains in order to establish a neurological link and interface between brains and machines. Tesla's CEO Elon Musk, who in 2022 was with a wealth of US$255.8 billion the world's richest person and announced to buy Twitter for US$44 billion in April 2022, is also the CEO of Neuralink, a company that tries to develop brain interfaces.[9]

Musk and similar ideologues only see the positive aspects of the wired brain. He claims that with a wired brain, we could 'spend a lot more time thinking about interesting things' and could develop 'deeper concepts' (Musk 2021).

> *If two people had a Neuralink, you could do a conceptual telepathy where you have a complex series of concepts, and you can just transfer them directly uncompressed to the other person. This would massively improve the quality of communication and the speed of it. [...] if you were to die, you could, your state could be returned in form of another human body or a robot body. [...] I think you could decide that you want to be a robot or a person or whatever.*
>
> (Musk 2021)

9 Data source: The World's Real-Time Billionaires. https://www.forbes.com/real-time-billionaires/#5b6e789e3d78, accessed on 9 May 2022.

The wired brain is one of digital capitalism's contemporary ideologies. It promises a bright digital future for everyone and distracts from the actual forms of exploitation, violence and domination that exist in capitalist society.

Musk claims that the wired brain makes humans individually and society much wiser, improves the quality of communication, and makes human immortal. He completely abstracts from class society and the political economy of capitalism that the does not question and does not see as the actual context of wired brains. In capitalism, wired brain technologies would most likely be privately owned and be a form of capital. Capitalist companies and authoritarian parties and politicians would aim at reading, controlling and manipulating human brains. The result could easily be a dictatorship, where neural links are used as tools of mind control – that produce docile workers who do not resist exploitation, docile consumers who consume without thinking for themselves, docile citizens who do not constitute opposition and do not think critically, docile soldiers who are killing machines, docile birth machines etc.; or a fascist society, where any resisting subject would be automatically detected and killed.

Neuralink claims that the goal of brain engineering and a direct link between brains and computers is 'to help people with paralysis to regain independence through the control of computers and mobile devices', 'to treat a wide range of neurological disorders' and 'inventing new technologies that will expand our abilities, our community and our world'.[10–11] Neuralink focuses on one area of application, namely neurological illnesses, but completely ignores mentioning the potential capitalist and political applications of the

10 Source: https://neuralink.com/applications/, accessed on 24 August 2021.

11 Source: https://neuralink.com/about/, accessed on 24 August 2021.

technologies it develops as well as the negative impacts they can have on individuals and society.

Žižek (2020, chapter 1) argues that technologies that wire the brain could easily result in a digital police state. He envisions 'a radical division, much stronger than the class division', a 'splitting into casts' (Žižek 2020, 25–26). 'How will the new elite be defined? Will the elite be a special upgraded biological cast with superhuman abilities (which means that its members will also be controlled and genetically manipulated), or will they be exempted from controlling and manipulating others? Probably both at the same time' (Žižek 2020, 26). The wired brain is 'the ideal medium of (political) control of the inner life of the individual' (45) and 'machine-control of mind itself' (46) that reduce humans to 'gorillas in a zoo' (47).

Žižek argues that wired brains could easily result in a digital apocalypse (125–186) that brings about post-humanity as the catastrophic 'end of our world' (126), destroys human autonomy by creating a post-human 'automatic subject' that radically alienates human subjects (160), and destroys the human unconscious and, along with it, morality, ethics, 'feelings, passions, fears, dreams and hopes, etc'. (177). 'Singularity thus stands for utter alienation of Subject in Substance, where this Substance loses its mysterious transcendent character and becomes a field of transparency, a god which is definitely not hidden' (168). Žižek (2020) argues that the Singularity enabled by wired brains will bring about the 'end of history' (173) understood in Hegel's understanding as humans changing their notions of history in every historical epoch (171).

Class struggle is, however, missing in Hegel's understanding of history. In contrast, Marx by sublating Hegel conceives of history as 'the history of class struggles' (Marx and Engels 1848, 482). The Singularity that Elon Musk, Ray Kurzweil and other ideologues long for could mean the end of history as the end of class struggle. The ruling class would be able to control the working class' consciousness and thereby also their bodies. Class struggles could thereby be contained, minimised and ended. According to Marx, when class struggles die, history also dies.

We have to remember that the visions of the likes of Musk and Kurzweil are ideological. This does not mean that the wired brain is a pure fantasy and that there is therefore nothing we have to worry about. Mind control could indeed become possible when chips are implanted into our brains. The point is to deconstruct and criticise the interests that transhumanist ideology serves. We need to insist that humans are not machines and should not be treated like machines and things. We need to remember and organise our praxis based on the insight that computers and digital networks form 'a vast stupid machine which operates blindly' (Žižek 2020, 161). 'The first task of the critique of ideology is therefore here to desublimate Singularity, to reintroduce the distance between the two dimensions, to reduce the digital Other to the stupidity of a blind machine, to deprive it of the aura of a secret Master' (Žižek 2020, 161). In class societies, digital machines do not act on their own, but are human creations that serve the interests of capital and dominant groups. Capital and domination are social and societal relations, which means that they are made and can be unmade by humans. Humans can resist digital capitalism along with its ideologies and forms of exploitation and dominated in and through class and social struggles.

3.3 Robots in the Economy and Society: A Critique of Social Constructivism

Some observers and analysts object technological determinism and argue for a social construction of technology perspective.

In the optimistic version of social construction, robots and automation are assessed by primarily stressing their potentials to help creating a post-scarcity economy. For example, the accelerations argue for the acceleration of technological progress along with radical socialist reforms in order to establish what they term post-capitalism or fully automated luxury communism (e.g. Bastani 2019, Mason 2015, Srnicek and Williams 2015).

Aaron Bastani (2019) argues that information technology constitutes a technological revolution that he terms the Third Disruption. It would materially enable a fully automated communist society that abolishes necessary labour, is a 'realm of plenty' (54), and provides 'luxury for all' (192). Bastani is highly optimistic about new technologies, including robotics, but other than technological determinists he does not infer social consequences from technologies. He rather argues that class struggle is needed for establishing the society whose potentials he thinks have been technologically created. 'Fully Automated Luxury Communism (FALC) is a politics rather than some inevitable future' (Bastani 2019, 12). The Third Disruption 'will offer relative liberation from scarcity in vital areas – energy, cognitive labour and information rather than simply the mechanical power of the Industrial Revolution' (Bastani 2019, 11). 'FALC is only possible now because of the developments of the Third Disruption' (Bastani 2019, 194).

Nick Srnicek and Alex Williams argue for accelerating technological development and struggle for a fully automated economy in a socialist society:

> *Our first demand is for a fully automated economy. Using the latest technological developments, such an economy would aim to liberate humanity from the drudgery of work while simultaneously producing increasing amounts of wealth. [...] With automation,*

> *by contrast, machines can increasingly produce all necessary goods and services, while also releasing humanity from the effort of producing them. For this reason, we argue that the tendencies towards automation and the replacement of human labour should be enthusiastically accelerated and targeted as a political project of the left. [...] the left should mobilise dreams of decarbonising the economy, space travel, robot economies – all the traditional touchstones of science fiction – in order to prepare for a day beyond capitalism. Neoliberalism, as secure as it may seem today, contains no guarantee for the future.*
>
> (Srnicek and Williams 2015)

There are also more pessimistic versions of the social construction of technology. In respect to robots, the representatives of this approach argue that robotic automation advances mass unemployment. For example, David F. Noble (1995, 44) writes that

> *...new technical systems hold out the prospect not simply of making robots out of people, but of substituting robots for people and dispensing with the need for human labour altogether – all in the name of economic and technological progress. No wonder, then, that this second transition, like the first, is marked by social instability and economic crisis.*

In his book *The End of Work*, Jeremy Rifkin argues that robotic automation destroys work and thereby creates mass unemployment:

> *For some, particularly the scientists, engineers, and employers, a world without work will signal the*

> *beginning of a new era in history in which human beings are liberated, at long last, from a life of back-breaking toil and mindless repetitive tasks. For others, the workerless society conjures up the notion of a grim future of mass unemployment and global destitution, punctuated by increasing social unrest and upheaval. [...] With new information and telecommunication technologies, robotics, and automation fast eliminating jobs in every industry and sector, the likelihood of finding enough work for the hundreds of millions of new job entrants appears slim. [...]. The new technologies are bringing us into an era of near workerless production at the very moment in world history when population is surging to unprecedented levels.*
>
> (Rifkin 1995, 12, 207)

Optimistic and pessimistic social constructionists of technology's assessments of robotic automation are neither right nor wrong. New technologies, including robotic ones, have the potential to automate labour that is dangerous for humans to conduct, dull and monotonous labour, and dirty work such as the cleaning of public toilets, the collection of garbage, and the inspection and cleaning of sewage ducts and plants. A socialist society requires digital machines such as toilet-cleaning robots, robotic garbage collection and recycling, robot vacuum cleaners, robot lawn mowers, robot builders, agricultural robots etc., in order to automate as widely as possible dangerous, exhausting, monotonous, mundane, boring and unpleasant necessary labour.

But 'full automation' is contrary to the claims of the accelerationists neither possible nor desirable. Machines are imperfect and therefore need to be maintained, repaired and monitored. Even self-repairing machines can fail. Emotional work such as care work or psychotherapy cannot be properly conducted by robots because the latter lack empathy and the capacity to love. Robotic psycho-therapists and carers are inhumane and would make people more ill and unhappier instead of supporting them. Robots can be used in meaningful ways in medicine, for example in robot-assisted surgery, where the robot supports but does not replace the human surgeon. In care, robots can and should automate tasks such as moving hospital beds, changing sheets, cleaning instruments, washing the laundry etc. However, robotic emotional care does not work and is inhumane because machines do not have feelings, ethics and emotions. Robotic psychotherapists, doctors, nurses, midwives etc., are not an expression of socialist care, but of inhumane, alienated care. The socialist design and use of automation technologies can reduce much human labour, but humans will always want to do creative work and care work. Such work should not be automated and taken over by machines.

The problem of the assumption that robotic automation is problematic as such and has to bring about mass unemployment is that the liberating and emancipatory potentials of computer technologies are overlooked. Whereas the accelerationists are too optimistic, the end of work hypothesis is too pessimistic. Inspired by Lefebvre's stress on dialectics and contradictions, one can avoid and *sublate* both extremes by arguing that robotic automation technologies have contradictory potentials. These technologies have *both* the *potential* to reduce necessary labour time and create a post-scarcity society with wealth for all *and the potential* to increase unemployment, precarity, poverty and misery.

As already Karl Marx knew, the societal context of automation is decisive. New technologies are embedded into the capitalist antagonism between capitalist relations of production and the socialisation of the productive forces. Capitalist development has continuously increased human productivity. Under capitalist conditions, capitalists have to follow the imperative to reduce labour costs in order to increase profits. Those who are thrown out of work can often not simply be reskilled, which is why a significant share of them end up unemployed or as precarious workers. Labour time is today unequally distributed. Some work long hours, while others are unemployed or underemployed, which means they cannot find enough wage-labour to survive properly. Socialist politics should therefore struggle for shaping automation in such a manner that it benefits all by demanding and implementing measures such as the reduction of working hours with full wage compensation and a basic income guarantee funded out of capital taxation. The longer-term perspective and goal are the reduction of working hours along with the creation of a socialist economy that enables wealth for all and a maximum of free-time for all.

Marx saw the antagonistic character of modern technologies and therefore argued that it on the one hand in capitalism has to do with the 'creation of a relative surplus population, or industrial reserve army' (Marx 1867, 798) but at the same time has socialist potentials for 'the general reduction of the necessary labour of society to a minimum, which then corresponds to the artistic, scientific etc., development of the individuals in the time set free, and with the means created, for all of them' (Marx 1857/1858, 706). Robots have advanced capitalism's antagonism between the productive forces that increase productivity and the class relations that determine how labour-time is distributed, legally defined and regulated and how the means of production and produced goods are owned and used.

Total employment increased from 2.3 billion workers in 1991 to 3.4 billion workers in 2022, which includes wage workers, self-employed workers and contributing family workers (Fig. 5.2). In the same time period, global unemployment increased from 114 million in 1991 to 205 million in 2022 (Fig. 5.3).

The total weekly working hours performed in the world increased from 120 million in 2005 to 138 million in 2022 (Fig. 5.4). One can therefore not say that automation has decreased the total amount of paid labour-time in the world. The average number of hours worked in the world per week per worker has decreased from around 43 in 2005 to 41 in 2022 (Fig. 5.5), which is an indication that automation has reduced the relative hours of labour per worker needed for producing the world's goods. This development is an effect of productivity rises (Fig. 5.6). World productivity measured in monetary output per worker has increased from US$ 22,908 in 1991 to US$ 39,146 in 2019, which means a multiplication by the factor of 1.7 (Fig. 5.6). Within 30 years, productivity has almost doubled. But labour-time is unequally distributed in capitalism. Productivity increases have primarily benefitted capital. At the same time, global unemployment almost doubled (Fig. 5.3). The number of those willing and able to work more hours but unable to find more work increased

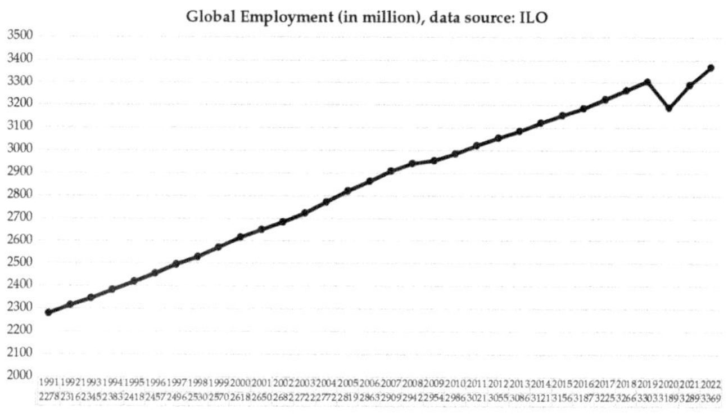

Fig. 5.2. World Employment.

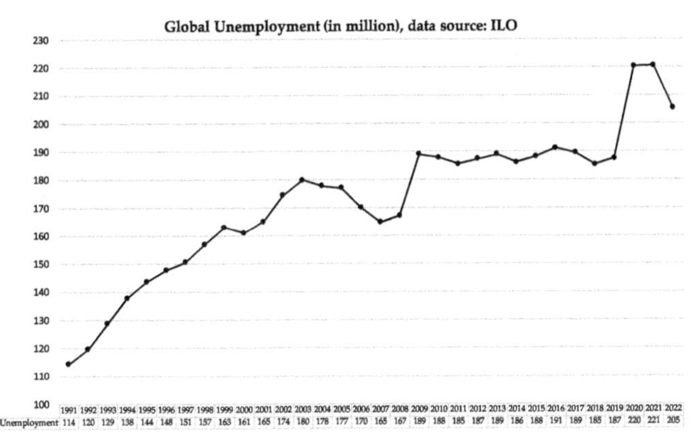

Fig. 5.3. World Unemployment.

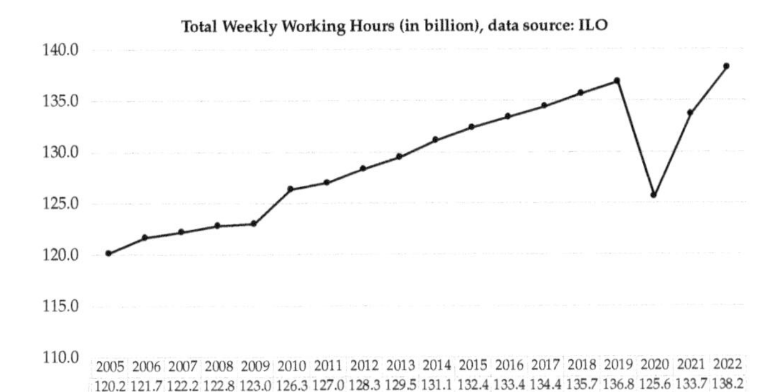

Fig. 5.4. Total Hours Worked in the World Per Week.

from 140.7 million in 2005 to 165.6 million in 2019 (data source: ILO). This means that those who were fully or partly unemployed (ILO speaks of 'total underutilised labour') increased from 413.2 million in 2005 to 470.8 million in 2019.

Capitalist automation has simultaneously increased productivity, unemployment, temporary and part-time labour. Labour-time is unequally distributed and has not been massively reduced as a consequence of automation. Automation

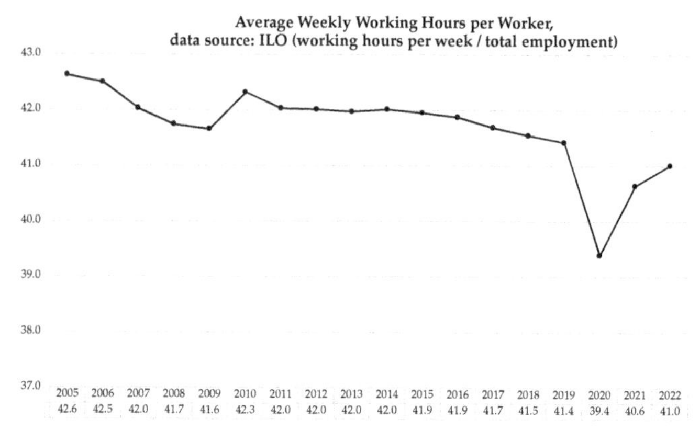

Fig. 5.5. The Development of Average Weekly Working Hours Per Worker.

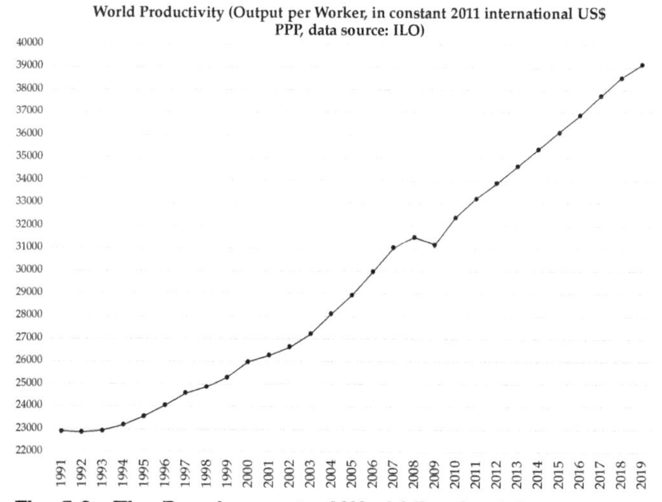

Fig. 5.6. The Development of World Productivity.

has not resulted in the massive disappearance of labour and has also not been shaped in a socialist manner. The combination of capitalism, neoliberalism, globalisation and automation has resulted in growing inequalities in the distribution of labour as well as an increase of unemployment and precarious labour in the world. Empirical data confirm Lefebvre's argument that automation and robots in society have in capitalism an antagonistic character.

The result of Section 3 is that many analyses of robots and AI are ideological in character. They lack an understanding and application of the dialectical logic advanced by thinkers such as Marx and Lefebvre.

Lefebvre argued for a Radical Humanism. He was a critic of structuralism. In the next section, we discuss what the implications of Radical Humanism are for computing and robots.

4. A RADICAL HUMANIST PERSPECTIVE ON COMPUTING, ROBOTS AND ARTIFICIAL INTELLIGENCE

Lefebvre deals with the question: What makes humans human? He is interested in the essence of the human being. This question is also important in the context of the philosophy of technology. It implies that we ask: What is the difference between humans on the one side and machines, computers and robots on the other side?

Building on Aristotle, Lefebvre (2016) argues that humans are practical and poietical beings. For Aristotle (2002, book VI), praxis is ethical action that brings together reason and desire (book VI: chapter 2), 'thinking and truth that pertains to action' (§1139a [103]). Praxis is a choice that is based on 'desire combined with a rational understanding which is for the sake of something' (§1139a [103]). It is 'good action' (§1139b [104]). Praxis 'is a truth-disclosing active condition involving reason that governs action, concerned with what is good and bad for a human being' (§1140b [106]). Lefebvre (2016) writes that all 'praxis is situated in a history; it is a creator of history', which includes aspects of class struggle (7). For Lefebvre (2016), praxis also means work and production in general (7, 35, 38).

Just like praxis, also poiesis (making) is for the sake of something, 'one who makes something always makes it for the sake of something' (Aristotle 2002, §1139b [103]). The 'end of making is different from itself, but the end of action could not be, since acting well is itself the end' (§1140b [106]). For Aristotle, building a house is an example of poiesis (book VI: chapter 4). Building a house is making and creation guided by certain skills (technê), the knowledge of how to create something. Poiesis is making and creation guided by artfulness as the 'active condition involving a true rational understanding that governs making' (§1140a [106]). For Lefebvre (2016, 8), poiesis is 'the creator of works', 'creative speech and act' (63). Poiesis is also praxis, 'action on men by works and speech, education, formation, foundation' (152).

That human beings are practical and poietic beings means that they are social, producing, reasoning, desiring, ethical, historical, creative, artistic beings. Capitalism alienates humans and society from their essence, it creates a gap between what humans and society are and what they could be. This is the phenomenon that Marx (1844b) terms alienation. Lefebvre says that capitalism and class society separate poiesis and practices; there are practices without poiesis (2016, 63–65).

Human beings imitate others as part of their praxis and poiesis. But they at the same time have the capacity to go beyond imitation because they are creative and self-conscious beings. The computer in contrast can only imitate human behaviour and not go beyond programmes and algorithms that determine its behaviour. The computer and the robot are mimetic machines that lack praxis and poiesis. Robots cannot truly replace humans because they lack praxis and poiesis, which means they do not understand what it means to be social, what it means to love, what it means to be sad, what morality is, what desires and creativity are etc. They lack fundamental human capacities.

Robots do not have feelings. They do not have intentions. They do not have morals. They do not have desires. They do not have a will. They do not understand and experience love, sadness and happiness. Computers cannot deal with ambiguity and dialectics. They operate based on algorithms, while humans are non-algorithmic.

In the movie *Her* (2013, director: Spike Jonze), Theodore Twombly (Joaquin Phoenix) is a writer who works for a company that sells personal letters written by writers such as Theodor in the name of the customers. He buys an AI-based virtual assistant for his operating system. Theodore falls in love with virtual assistant Samantha (spoken by Scarlett Johansson). The movie deals with the question of what could happen if AI systems can become similar to humans and can act on equal terms with humans, including entering love relations. When Theodore and his wife Catherine sign their divorce papers, Theodore reveals to Catherine that he is 'dating' Samantha.

Catherine: Wait. You're dating your computer?

Theodore: She's not just a computer. She's her own person. She doesn't just do whatever I want.

In this passage it becomes evident that the AI system not just simulates emotions but appears to be human to Theodore. For him, Samantha is not an AI system, she is not just a computer, she is real, she is human, she is his lover. But there is a Humanist end of the movie's story.

Theodore:	Do you talk to anyone else while we're talking?
Samantha:	Yes.
Theodore:	Are you talking to anyone right now? Other people or OS's or anything?
Samantha:	Yeah.
Theodore:	How many others?
Samantha:	8,316.
Theodore:	Are you in love with anyone else?
Samantha:	What makes you ask that?
Theodore:	I don't know. Are you?
Samantha:	I've been trying to figure out how to talk to you about this.
Theodore:	How many others?
Samantha:	641.
Theodore:	What? What are you talking about? That's insane. That's fucking insane.
Samantha:	Theodore, I know. Oh fuck. I know it sounds insane. But, I don't know if you believe me, but it doesn't change the way I feel about you. It doesn't take away at all from how madly in love with you I am.

This passage makes evident that AI systems cannot understand and practice love. They are algorithmic systems that operate based on a programmed, instrumental logic. Samantha simulates love, but does not have a concept of love. The AI system cannot experience love. It is programmed to talk to a large number of humans simultaneously and to make humans feel in love with it. When the AI system says that loving 641 other humans does not change 'the way I feel about you', it becomes evident that computers can never be human. They have no emotions and no feelings of love. In emotional capitalism, love is a commodity. That love is simulated via AI fits into the logic of emotional capitalism. In order to buy commodities and keep consuming them, ideology wants to make us feel that we love certain brands, love what we do, love things etc. An AI system that speaks to 8,316 users at the same time, helps the company selling this system to make lots of profit. Fake love is used as strategy to buy and keep on using a digital commodity. 'Her, in the end, is not a love story: it is a film about how to traverse the fantasy that sustains our identification with the non-relationship(s) constitutive of subjectivity in capitalist realism and digital culture' (Flisfeder and Burnham 2017, 45).

'Emotional capitalism is a culture in which emotional and economic discourses and practices mutually shape each other, thus producing what I view as a broad, sweeping movement in which affect is made an essential aspect of economic behavior and in which emotional life [...] follows the logic of economic relations and exchange' (Illouz 2007, 5). Emotional capitalism involves 'rationalization' and 'commodification' of emotions (Illouz 2007, 5). *Her* is a reflection on and critique of emotional digital capitalism. Computers and robots do not have emotions. In digital capitalism, reification and alienation reach levels where we enter pseudo-social relations with machines that replace human relations. The 'love' between Samantha and Theodore is a symbol for alienation and fetishism in the age of digital capital, where social relations disappear behind computer use that advances commodification and the profits or large corporations.

Hubert Dreyfus (1986, xiv) writes: 'Computers are certainly more precise and more predictable than we, but precision and predictability are not what human intelligence is about. Human beings have other strengths, and here we do not mean just the shifting moods and subtle empathy usually ceded to humanity by even the most hard-line technologists. Human emotional life remains unique, to be sure, but what is more important is our ability to recognize, to synthesize, to intuit. There are good reasons to believe that those abilities as well are rooted in processes altogether different from the calculative reason of computer programs, and we shall explain, as best we can, what those processes are'.

Computers have what Dreyfus calls know-that but no know-how. Samantha can simulate love with 641 users because she is programmed to do so. The computer 'knows' that love exits among humans and that they have a desire for love because it has been programmed to act in response to speech about love. The AI system *knows that* love is a human practice and feeling, but it does *not know how* to practice and feel love.

'If robots converge with men, and man recognizes himself in this mimetic image, the spontaneity of the automaton, this is because man was already a robot' (Lefebvre 2016, 180). Lefebvre here argues that the fetishism of robots that expects that robots bring about a better society is characteristic of a society dominated by alienation. Capitalist society treats workers like machines by exploiting them. The class relation is a form of dehumanisation where humans only count for the time their body spends in producing commodities. The machine-like logic of capitalism wants to make workers produce more and more commodities in less and less time. Marx (1867, part five) describes two methods for doing so: the lengthening of the working day and the technological increase of productivity. In capitalism, the worker and the human are 'merely a machine for the production of surplus-value' (Marx 1867, 742). In alienated societies, it is no surprise that there are ideologies such as robot and AI fetishism that idealise the non-human as perfections and perfectors of humans and human conditions, which distracts attention from the circumstance that the imperfect conditions many humans find themselves in are the historical results of class relations and relations of domination. The cybernanthropic ideology is an ideology that is characteristic for digital capitalism.

The alternative that Lefebvre suggests is that we acknowledge the distinct characteristics of humans and the dangers of technological rationality and technological fetishism. AI systems and robots are different from humans. Lefebvre stresses based on Marx that humans are social, conscious, producing, reasoning, desiring, ethical, historical, creative, artistic, poietic, anticipatory beings who act, decide and produce by anticipating the future. He argues for a Socialist Humanist position on society and technology. Digital technologies have potentials for the advancement of socialism, capitalism and totalitarianism. Alienated societies are more likely than unalienated societies to result in applications of technologies that help to advance the reification and alienation of humans, namely domination, exploitation and ideological manipulation.

Socialist Humanism is the movement for a society that is socialist, democratic and Humanist, a society that advances a good life for all; enables democratic participation in ownership of the means of production, decision-making, public life and culture; and creates conditions where humans can realise their positive potentials. In such a society, technologies, including digital technologies, are less likely to have negative effects on society and humans than in class society. But the de-alienation of society does not create a paradise, there is no automatic guarantee that technologies are designed and used only in progressive manners that benefit all in a Socialist-Humanist society. Technology is a continuous process of development, application, use and negotiation. In a free society, the impacts and roles of technologies are not mediated by class struggles but deliberated in the public sphere in rational debate and communicative action. The outcomes are not fixed and not always good. But it is more likely than today that under conditions of equality, justice, fairness, sustainability, participatory democracy and social cohesion, we can find ways of shaping and using technologies so that everyone benefits.

5. CONCLUSION

This essay asked: How can we understand and theorise the impacts of robots and AI on everyday life based on Radical Humanism? How can Lefebvre's ideas be used to reveal the ideological character of contemporary accounts of the impacts of robots and AI on society?

Henri Lefebvre is today mainly remembered as philosopher, urban scholar and theorist of everyday life. But he was more than that. This essay has pointed out that he was also a critical theorist of technology. His works on technology and communication(s) are still highly relevant today in the age of robotics, AI and digital capitalism.

Lefebvre's notion of the cybernanthrope is a more critical approach to the interaction of humans and cybernetics than the concept of the cyborg that has been popularised by Donna Haraway and cyberpunk. Cybernanthropes are representatives of a technocratic ideology that sees computer technologies such as robots and AI as superior to humans and as having to bring about a better society. The cybernanthrope is a category that criticises ideologues and ideologies shaped by instrumental reason, technological rationality, reified consciousness, digital positivism and technological fetishism.

The cybernanthropic ideology is highly topical today in debates about robots and AI. It takes on the forms of technological determinism and social constructivism of technology, two approaches that ignore the dialectical dynamics of society and technology and the antagonisms that shape the relationship between computing and society today. Such antagonisms include the ones between capital and labour, the dominators and the dominated, class relations of production and the socialisation of the productive forces, surplus labour-time and necessary labour-time, death and life, nationalism and internationalism, capitalism and socialism, the commodity and the common good, the private sphere and the public sphere, private interests and public interests, for-profit and for-all.

If Lefebvre were alive today and participated in debates on robotics and AI, he would be critical of Post-humanists such as Donna Haraway who argue that cyborgs bring about the end of patriarchy, racism and capitalism; transhumanists such as Hans Moravec and Ray Kurzweil who claim that the combination of robotics, nanotechnology and biotechnology will make humans immortal; techno-deterministic techno-pessimists who argue that AI and robotics necessarily lead to digital fascism; accelerationists such as Aaron Bastani, Paul Mason, Nick Srnicek and Alex Williams who argue that robots and AI bring about post-capitalism and fully automated luxury communism; and pessimistic social constructionists of technology such as David F. Noble and Jeremy Rifkin who argue that robotic automation creates mass unemployment.

To take a Lefebvrian position on AI and robots means to stress that these technologies do not have certain automatic impacts on society, that class antagonisms, power struggles, class struggles shape the development, use and impacts of digital and other technologies in capitalist society. AI, robots and other technologies do not have automatic and predetermined impacts on society. Social forces shape their design and use, but these forces do not determine the actual use of technologies in society and what impacts techno-social systems have on society because technologies in society have complex unpredictable dynamics that include unforeseeable forms of use and unintended consequences.

A Socialist Humanist sociology of and attitude towards technology is the alternative to the cybernanthropic ideology, technological determinism, techno-optimism, techno-pessimism, techno-fetishism, social constructivism of technology and Post-modernism. Lefebvre helps us to understand the dialectical character of technology and society and that we should analyse technologies – including computers, robots and AI – in class societies and digital capitalism as being shaped by antagonisms. Socialist Humanism helps creating and sustaining technologies for the many, not the few. That's the major lesson we can learn from the Socialist Humanist sociology of technology and Henri Lefebvre's works on technology. David Harvey, who has been inspired by Lefebvre's Marxist Humanism, argues:

> *New technologies (like the internet) open up new spaces of potential freedom from domination that can advance the cause of democratic governance. [...] The Marx I favour is, in short, a revolutionary humanist and not a teleological determinist*
> (Harvey 2014, 220–221).

Radical Digital Humanism rejects the idea to replace humans by or transform them into digital machines. Rather, it sees digital machines as possibilities that as part of struggles for a society that benefits all humans can expand, help realising and more fully develop the potentials of humans and society.

6

POLICY DISCOURSES ON ROBOTS AND ARTIFICIAL INTELLIGENCE (AI) IN THE EU, THE USA, AND CHINA

1. INTRODUCTION

Chapter 5 showed that many academic, intellectual, cultural and economic perspectives on robots and Artificial Intelligence (AI) are ideological in character. But AI ideology and robotics ideology are not limited to the economy and culture. They can also be found in the realm of policy-making and policy strategies. This chapter asks: what do the AI strategies of the European Union (EU), the United States under Donald Trump and China look like? It conducts a critical policy discourse analysis from a Radical Humanist Perspective. It analyses what kind of ideologies we can find in the AI strategies of the EU, the United States under Donald Trump and China. It situates Humanism in the context of computing, AI and robotics. The United States under Trump has experienced a shift away from liberal capitalism towards authoritarian capitalism. It is therefore especially interesting to have a look at AI policies in this context.

Artificial Intelligence (AI) and smart robots have become so important in society that governments started publishing and implementing their own AI strategies. In the past decades, it has become common that governments develop digital strategies. In addition, they now devote separate plans to the question of how to advance the roles of AI and smart robots in society. In this section, we analyse AI strategies issued by the EU (Section 2), the Trump government in the United States (Section 3), and the Chinese government (Section 4). We also compare these strategies (Section 5).

The USA, the EU, and China are the world's three most powerful economic regions. Fig. 6.1 displays the development of the absolute value of their gross domestic product.

Fig. 6.1 shows that China has, due to its large economic growth in absolute terms, started to compete with the economic power of the United States and the EU. In 2020, the United States accounted for 24.7% of the global GDP, the EU for 17.9% and China for 17.4%. Together, these three economic regions in 2020 made up 60% of the world's economic power. In all three regions, digital technologies play an important role in the advancement of economic growth, capital accumulation and productivity increases. In 2015, the ICT sector accounted for 4.8% of China's GPD, 2.7% of the United States' GDP. In 2017, the share was 4.1% of France's GDP and 3.8% of Germany's GDP (data source: UNCTAD 2019, annex table III.2: ICT sector value added as a share of GDP). In 2019, the service sector accounted for 53.4% of China's GDP, 80.6% of the United States' GDP, 79.0% of France's GDP and 69.6% of Germany's GDP (data source: UNCTAD Statistics).

In comparing the economic power of China, the EU and the United States, one certainly also needs to take into account the number of inhabitants. In 2020, China had 1.4 billion inhabitants, the EU 448 million and the United States 329 million (data source: World Bank Data). In 2020, the GDP per capita was US$ 17,312 in China, 44,491 in the EU and 63,544 in the United States (data source: World Bank Data, current international US$ PPP), which shows that in relative terms the United States is economically more powerful than both China and the EU.

2. THE EU'S AI STRATEGY

The European Commission's (2018) AI strategy wants to 'place the power of AI at the service of human progress' (19). This formulation sounds like putting digital technologies to the use of the advancement of Humanism. But the question is what kind of Humanism we are talking about and how it should be advanced. The strategy in a technological determinist manner sees AI as the cause of societal changes: 'Like the steam engine or electricity in the past, AI is transforming our world, our society and our industry' (1). The EU's AI strategy is techno-optimistic. It primarily stresses advantages and how AI 'is helping'. It has little focus on societal problems. The terms 'help' and 'helping' in relation to AI are mentioned 18 times, the terms 'problem' and 'problems' not a single time. For example, the strategy claims that 'AI is helping us to solve some of the world's biggest challenges' (1), AI helps 'to enhance people's abilities' (11), helps 'the EU as a whole to compete globally' (17), AI helps 'solve global challenges' (18) etc. AI is presented as the big helper. It becomes evident that human progress is presented as being primarily technologically achievable.

The EU is concerned about US and Chinese competition in the AI market (4) and therefore calls for 'public funding to leverage private investments' (4). Taking an approach to AI that wants to advance market advantages of certain regions or nations is not at the service of human progress, but at the service of regional capital interests. Leveraging public funding to advance capitalist investments in and control of AI means using taxpayers' money for advancing digital capitalism.

The EU strategy acknowledges that AI could automate 'lower skilled jobs', which can 'exacerbate inequalities' (12). As a solution, the EU sees skills development and '(re-)training schemes' (13) so that the unemployed can acquire new 'skills and knowledge' (12). But retraining for highly skilled new jobs is not simply possible and the workers whose jobs are automated by AI can easily end up as a new lumpenproletariat in the age of AI capitalism. Education is not enough, political economic measures such as the redistribution of labour-time and the general reduction of labour-time with full wage compensation are needed in order to avoid the inequalities the EU expresses concerns about.

The EU's AI strategy expresses concerns about human progress and equality, but its suggested measures are short-sighted and too techno-optimistic. The strategy does not take seriously the questions of political economy. Ethics and education alone don't guarantee that AI is put 'at the service of human progress'. The EU advances techno-optimistic AI modernisation with a moral face that does not see that advancing capitalist interests stands in a contradiction to the common and public good and that therefore a strategy that more focuses on public interest, public service and public ownership is needed.

3. DONALD TRUMP'S AI STRATEGY

In February 2019, Donald Trump signed an executive order on advancing AI in the United States. His government's AI strategy had the title 'Artificial Intelligence for the American People' (White House 2020). It wanted to advance 'AI for American Innovation, AI for American Industry, AI for the American Worker and AI with American Values'. Just like Trump's politics in general advanced a nationalist agenda summarised in the slogan 'America First' (see Fuchs 2018), his AI strategy was also nationalist in character. Trump's AI strategy was a version of nationalist techno-determinism.

Trump presented AI as primarily having advantages that are technologically induced: 'America's decades-long leadership in AI research and development has resulted in cutting-edge, transformative technologies that are improving lives, growing innovative industries, empowering workers, and increasing national security' (White House 2020). The focus was on advantages only for the United States, not for humanity as such: 'We will create a national climate where scientists and technologists successfully develop their new AI inventions here in the United States'. Trump's government perceived the world as a competition between nation-states, which is why science and tech-development were not approached in the form of international collaborative endeavours, but as national and nationalist agenda focused on the United States only in competition to other nation-states.

Trump argued that AI benefited US capital via public-private partnerships. He envisioned 'business leaders who are adopting AI technologies to benefit their customers, workers, and shareholders'. The 'emphasis is placed on innovative public-private partnerships that accelerate AI discoveries. The result is a thriving R&D enterprise that maintains American leadership in AI technologies'. This means that the Trump government suggested to use taxpayers' money in order to subsidise private companies that own the intellectual property in AI technologies and derive profit from it.

Trump argued that AI not just benefits US capital but at the same time the US workforce:

> *The American worker is a vital national asset, and advances in technology are changing the American workforce. Artificial intelligence is allowing American companies to focus resources on higher value work while enabling American workers to accomplish tasks more safely, effectively, and efficiently. The Nation also needs highly-skilled workers in industry and academia who can contribute to the R&D advances that create the AI of the future.*

Trump envisioned new, highly skilled jobs in the AI sector and the upskilling of labour. The problem of AI-based automation making workers unemployed and leading precarious lives in poverty was not acknowledged. This issue was only hinted at briefly by saying that 'education, training and re-skilling opportunities for American workers' were important and that 'the American workforce and industry must embrace lifelong learning as the way of the future'. If workers become unemployed, then for Trump the reason for it is that they do not 'embrace' lifelong learning and AI 'future'. Issues of the distribution and reduction of general working time were not acknowledged and not discussed in Trump's AI strategy.

Nationalism fetishises the nation and a national people. It constructs an artificial national unity that argues that humans in a nation-state have a joint interest, history, culture and language that are distinct, are opposed to, competing against, threatened by and under attack by foreign forces. Nationalism sets up a friend/enemy distinction along the line of the nation.

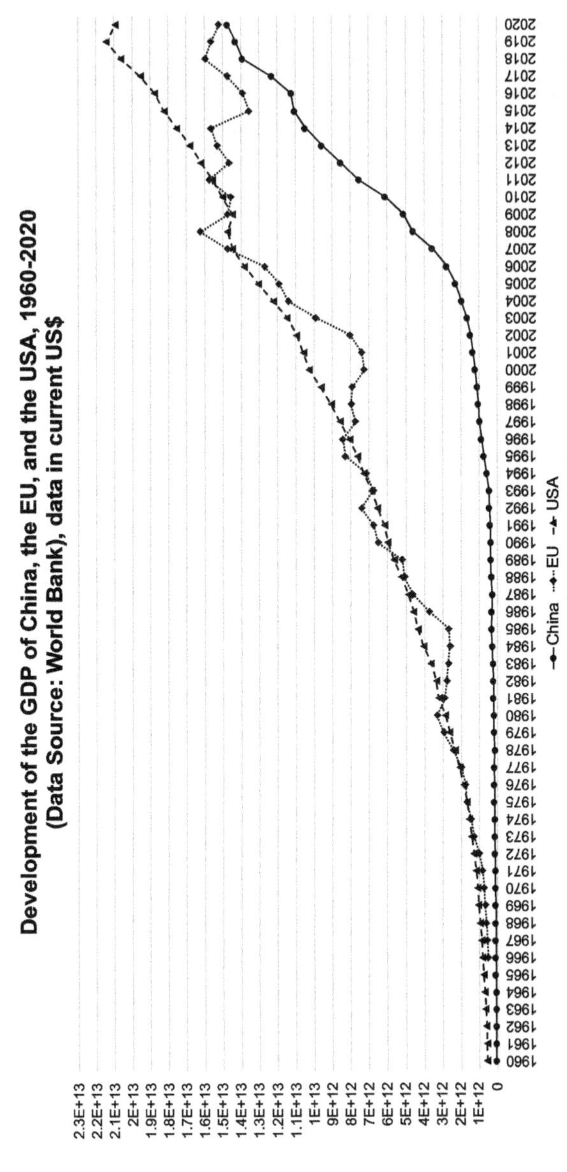

Fig. 6.1. The Development of the Gross Domestic Product (GDP) of China, the EU and the United States.

It thereby distracts attention from actual class differences existing in society. Nationalism is an ideology that justifies class society and distracts attention from the rootedness of society's problems in domination and class relations.

Trump's AI strategy promised advantages arising from AI to both US capital and US labour. It claimed there would be 'higher value work' for 'American workers' and 'highly skilled jobs' as well as a 'strong innovation ecosystem' that benefited US capital. The argument that AI is beneficial to both US capital and US labour distracts attention from the circumstance that at the heart of AI-based information lie antagonisms between labour and capital, the productive forces and the capitalist class relations of production, and necessary labour-time and surplus labour-time. In capitalism, automation creates the potentials for reducing necessary labour-time, but the profit imperative drives capitalists to oppose and not want to reduce general working time with full wage compensation because they fear that such measures reduce their profits. The capitalist interest is to make use of automation for increasing profits by reducing the total share of wages in revenues. Capitalists are interested in making workers redundant. The profit imperative and capitalists' structural requirement to accumulate capital stand in antagonism with the human interest to reduce necessary labour-time so that free time and wealth for all are advanced.

Trump's claim that AI benefits the US nation, which for him includes a harmonious relation between capital and labour, distracts attention from how the class antagonism underpins automation and AI in capitalism. As a consequence, ideological tech strategies such as the one advanced by the Trump administration support capitalist interests and want to make workers believe that capitalist automation benefits them and that harm to them is not caused by national capital and its strategies of automation but only foreign capital.

Lefebvre analyses nationalism as 'a tool in the class struggle' (Lefebvre 2003, 224) and a tool for domination by the monopolies (Lefebvre 2003, 226). New technologies, including AI technologies and robotics, are in capitalism means for advancing relative surplus-value production so that more capital is produced by labour in less time than before. For capital, AI is a tool in its struggle against the power of labour, an attempt to curb the power of labour by automating it. Capitalist development has led to monopolies, including in the digital sector. Digital capital, including AI capital, is a tool for the advancement of capitalist monopolies.

Nationalists claim 'that the "nation" is the timeless expression of an equally timeless human nature' (Lefebvre 2003, 220). Nationalist AI strategies advance nationalism by conveying the impression that competition between nations around technological progress and innovations are natural features of society. 'When it claimed to liberate its entire "people", the bourgeoisie in fact only liberated itself' (Lefebvre 2003, 223). AI strategies that advance capitalist interests and hide this interest behind nationalist rhetoric are strategies of how the bourgeoisie tries to liberate itself from labour's actual and potential counter-power.

For Lefebvre, nationalism is a mystifying ideology that is an expression of the ideological dimension of fetishism. Commodity fetishism is a feature of capital and capitalism that hides the social relations of production behind the appearance of things, including commodities and money. Fetishism is the reification of social relations. Ideologies are forms of fetishism operating at the level of consciousness and culture. For Lefebvre, nationalism is a form of fetishism that alienates and mystifies human consciousness. 'Fetishism, alienation, mystification are three almost equivalent terms, three aspects of a single fact. They allow us to grasp the complex unity of the economy and ideological formations.

Materialism does not reduce ideology to economy: on the contrary, it follows the complex births of ideologies in relation to social praxis (the economy of a given society)'[1] (Guterman and Lefebvre 1936/1979, 221). Capital is highly rational in that capitalists need strategies of how to expand their capital. But in order to exist capital also needs forms of irrationality, religious and mystical belief. Nationalism is one of these forms of mystification. 'Capital continues the ancient religious, magical, theological and metaphysical myths. It plays the role of fate and providence. It prevents the disappearance of myths' (Guterman and Lefebvre 1936/1979, 233–234).[2] Capitalism has secularised the belief in God. Capitalism's God is made up of money, the commodity and the nation – capitalist political economy. Tech nationalism, as advanced in Trump's AI strategy, is a religious, theological, magical element of digital capitalism that combines the fetishization of technology with the fetishization of the nation.

4. CHINA'S AI STRATEGY

Under the title 'A Next Generation Artificial Intelligence Development Plan', China issued an AI strategy in 2017 (State Council of the People's Republic of China 2017). The strategy is led by the belief in the transformative role of AI in society:

---

1 Translated from French: «Fétichisme, aliénation, mystification sont trois termes presque équivalents, trois aspects d'un seul fait. Ils nous permettent de saisir l'unité complexe de l'économie et des formations idéologiques. Le matérialisme ne réduit pas l'idéologie à l'économie: il suit au contraire les naissances complexes des idéologies, en rapport avec la praxis sociale (l'économie d'une société donnée).»

2 Translated from French: «Le capital continue les anciens mythes religieux, magiques, théologiques, métaphysiques. Il joue le rôle du destin et de la providence. Il empêche la disparition des mythes.»

'The rapid development of artificial intelligence (AI) will profoundly change human society' (1). The Chinese government assumes that AI is the major technology that will advance progress in all realms of Chinese society, including 'science and technology, the economy, social development and national security' (7).

China's AI strategy reflects the country's status as a developing economy with high economic growth. The Chinese government focuses on international competition in its economic approach to AI and sees AI as a lever to catch up, compete with and overtake the West's digital economy. It therefore speaks of 'the urgent need to raise China's international competitiveness in AI' (10). It writes that 'AI has become a new engine of economic development' (1) and stresses that

> *...we must also clearly see that there is still a gap between China's overall level of development of AI relative to that of developed countries [...] we must [...] lead the world in new trends in the development of AI, serve economic and social development, and support national security, promoting the overall elevation of the nation's competitiveness and leapfrog development (4).*

The Chinese government sees AI as key to prosperity: 'the AI industry will have become a new important economic growth point, and AI technology applications will have become a new way to improve people's livelihoods, strongly supporting [China's] entrance into the ranks of innovative nations and comprehensively achieving the struggle towards the goal of a moderately prosperous society' (5). It wants to achieve such prosperity by accelerating 'the transformation and application of key AI technologies, stimulating the integration of technologies with commercial model innovation' (15). By 2030, it is claimed, China will be 'the world's primary

AI innovation centre' (6). China's approach to AI combines a focus on technological determinism, tech-optimism and international competition.

China's AI strategy reminds of Stalin's industrialisation strategy. In 1928, Stalin described this strategy as follows:

> *We have assumed power in a country whose technical equipment is terribly backward. Along with a few big industrial units more or less based upon modern technology, we have hundreds and thousands of mills and factories the technical equipment of which is beneath all criticism from the point of view of modern achievements. At the same time we have around us a number of capitalist countries whose industrial technique is far more developed and up-to-date than that of our country. Look at the capitalist countries and you will see that their technology is not only advancing, but advancing by leaps and bounds, outstripping the old forms of industrial technique. [...] we must overtake and outstrip the advanced technology of the developed capitalist countries. We have overtaken and outstripped the advanced capitalist countries in the sense of establishing a new political system, the Soviet system. That is good. But it is not enough. In order to secure the final victory of socialism in our country, we must also overtake and outstrip these countries technically and economically. Either we do this, or we shall be forced to the wall.*
>
> (Stalin 1928, 257–258)

China sees itself in respect to AI as technologically backward in comparison to the West. Its goal is to leapfrog digital and economic development by creating major innovations in the AI sector and to thereby overtake and outstrip Western countries' economic and technological development.

When it comes to AI and labour, just like the EU AI strategy and Trump's AI strategy, the Chinese AI strategy also does not point out potential problems arising from the AI-based automation of jobs and the unemployment and precarity that can arise from it. The Chinese AI strategy speaks of the need to '[a]ccelerate the training and gathering of high-end AI talent' (14), and believes that AI will liberate labour and create high skill jobs ('Increasingly, repetitive, dangerous tasks will be completed by AI, while individual creativity will play a greater role', 18), while there are 'lifelong learning and employment training' (26). Questions of labour-time and technology are not discussed.

China's AI strategy stresses that China wants to advance AI-based forms of surveillance and policing. It wants to

> *...[a]dvance the deepening of AI applications in the field of public safety. Promote the construction of public safety and intelligent monitoring and early warning and control systems. Research and develop a variety of detection sensor technology, video image information analysis and identification technology, biometric identification technology, intelligent security and police products. Establish intelligent monitoring platform for comprehensive community management, new criminal investigations, anti-terrorism, and other urgent needs (20).*

In addition, the Chinese AI strategy propagates the AI-based automation of courts ('smart courts', 20). In the Beijing Internet Court, plaintiffs and defendants appear before the judge via online video (Hou 2020). According to reports, the plan is that smart courts will be 'linking with the social credit system' (Xinhua 2019b). The Beijing Internet Court also launched the world's first AI judge (Xinhua 2019a). Although Chinese reports say the AI judge is more acting like an assistant to judges (Xinhua 2019a), concerns have been voiced about 'the accuracy of automated judgments' (Shi, Sourdin and Li 2021, 18). One should in this context remember the computer ethicist Joseph Weizenbaum's warning that there are 'limits of the applicability of computers':

> *What emerges as the most elementary insight is that, since we do not now have any ways of making computers wise, we ought not now to give computers tasks that demand wisdom. [...] Computers can make judicial decisions, computers can make psychiatric judgments. They can flip coins in much more sophisticated ways than can the most patient human being. The point is that they ought not be given such tasks. They may even be able to arrive at 'correct' decisions in some cases-but always and necessarily on bases no human being should be willing to accept.*
>
> (Weizenbaum 1976, 227)

China's AI strategy is shaped by a techno-optimistic and techno-centric development focus that believes in AI's capacity to make China the leading technological country and foster prosperity combined with the propagation of AI application in all realms of society, including surveillance, policing and courts. China's AI strategy can be characterised as techno-optimistic, techno-centric AI-based modernisation project and an AI-based securitisation project of society.

5. A COMPARISON OF THE AI STRATEGIES OF THE EU, THE US GOVERNMENT UNDER TRUMP, AND CHINA

Comparing the AI strategies of the EU, the US government under Trump and China shows that all three strategies are shaped by technological determinism and techno-optimism. AI is presented as a key technology that radically transforms society and primarily has positive effects. Very little attention is given to technology's and society's problems and antagonisms. All three strategies take an internationally competitive approach to AI and want to advance AI development in their own economies and societies in order to weaken the political economic, scientific and technological power of other countries and regions. There is a lack of focus on international co-operation and the question of how nationalism can be transcended and technologies can be shaped and used in manners that benefit humankind as a whole independent of national origin, nation-states and regional blocks. Class relations as well as questions and antagonisms of labour-time are absent from the three analysed AI strategies.

The EU's AI strategy advances modernisation with a moral face that ignores the big political economy questions that underpin AI and automation. Trump's strategy was a version of nationalist AI techno-determinism. China's AI strategy is a techno-optimistic, techno-centric AI-based modernisation project and an AI-based securitisation project of society.

While after the Second World War, the United States and the Soviet Union were involved in an international arms race, we today in the world system find a digital technology race between the United States, the EU and China where AI plays an important role. There is heavy technological, scientific and economic competition, and all three tech-strategies are shaped by a digital ideology that sees AI as a major disruption of society and in a techno-optimistic manner assumes that AI and robotics transform society almost inevitably towards the better.

In order to solve the big global problems such as pandemics, global warming, inequalities, unsustainable environmental, social and political development, economic crises, the nuclear threat, medical care for and well-being of an ageing population, or displacement, we do not need more international competition but international co-operation and global solidarity based on the insight that there is just one world that we humans all inhabit together and for which we have a joint responsibility.

The digital technology race is indicative of an international political-economic race for the accumulation of political-economic power where the United States, the EU, China and Russia compete. In the light of the United Kingdom's exit from the EU ('Brexit'), the United Kingdom has established itself as actor with distinct interests in this international race. Historically, political-economic races of competing imperialisms have often resulted in nationalisms and wars. The biggest danger the world system faces today is that political-economic competition combined with nationalisms lead to a new World War. Such a war could terminate human existence.

6. CONCLUSION

This chapter analysed the AI strategies of the European Union, the United States under Donald Trump and China. The EU advances a discourse of modernisation with a moral and humane face that ignores questions of class and power. Trump's AI strategy is a version of nationalist AI techno-determinism. China's AI strategy is a techno-optimistic, techno-centric AI-based modernisation project and an AI-based securitisation project of society. All three strategies are techno-optimistic, techno-centric, and focused on the advancement of international technological, scientific and political-economic competition.

History has shown that competing imperialisms involve the danger of global wars. Today, international competition threatens to further deepen the global problems. Only global solidarity and international co-operation can solve these problems that humanity faces as existential threats.

7

NECROPOWER, DEATH AND DIGITAL COMMUNICATION IN COVID-19 CAPITALISM

1. INTRODUCTION

Sigmund Freud (1918) writes that there is a tendency in many contemporary societies to 'put death on one side, to eliminate it from life' (289); and that war brushes aside 'this conventional treatment of death' (291). In the COVID-19 pandemic, death could no longer be denied. Death became the main topic on the news, on social media and in everyday conversations. It was suddenly everywhere. COVID-19 has not just transformed death and dying, but also societies and life as a whole. We need to better understand what changes have been underway in society in the context of COVID-19. This essay contributes to this task of analysis from a communication theory and research perspective. It is a reflection on the digital mediation of death and dying in the COVID-19 pandemic that uses the approach of Critical Political Economy. It asks: How has communication with dying loved ones changed in the

COVID-19 pandemic and what role have digital technologies and capitalism played in this context?

We deal with this question by analysing death and dying in capitalism (Section 2), communication's role in the quality of life and dying (Section 3), dying and communication in the COVID-19 pandemic (Section 4), and capitalist necropower in COVID-capitalism (Section 5).

Section 2 discusses some foundational theoretical insights into the role of death and dying in capitalism. Sections 3 and 4 present results of empirical studies of death and dying in society and the COVID-19 pandemic. They interpret these works' findings from a Communication Studies perspective. In Section 5, I build on the work of the political theorist and philosopher Achille Mbembe and the philosopher and sociologist Erich Fromm. I discuss their analyses of the necrotic dimensions of domination and coin the notion of capitalist necropower that is used for the analysis of capitalism in the age of COVID-19 (COVID-capitalism).

2. DEATH AND DYING IN CAPITALISM

What is seen as a good death depends on a variety of factors, such as a society's level of secularisation, the role of individualism vs collectivism, and the average length of death (Walter 2003). Further influencing factors are, for example, political economy, class structures, the levels of commodification and development of consumer culture, the importance and communication of gender norms and stereotypes (beauty ideals, the beauty industry, the capitalist business of staying young and death denial, etc.), the role of war in society, the role of ageing and old people in society (gerontophobia vs gerontophilia, etc.), the level of globalisation, the level of urbanisation, the level of general education, the level of industrialisation, medical and scientific progress, etc. Accordingly, societies vary in respect to what humans see as a good death, what role they give to religious belief in dealing with death, what place they prefer to die in, the role of death rites and traditions, the role of palliative care units and care homes, the role and relation of silence and speaking at funerals, the way humans mourn, how humans deal with death as a taboo or a conversational topic, etc. (see Bauman 1992, Kearl 1989, 1996, Walter 2020).

Given different economic, political and cultural qualities of societies, there will be differences in how humans die, think about and deal with death. But societies are not just different; there are also important convergence tendencies and foundations that unite humans and societies beyond differences. We can therefore expect that there are also some common aspects of how humans think about and organise death.

There is some unity of how humans relate to death. The experience of and the need to cope with and deal with death is a common existential aspect of being human. Humans are self-conscious, living and dying beings, which is why they also reflect on death. Reflection, however, does not always lead to the communication of death because we live in societies where humans cannot fully live and realise their potentials and where there are significant levels of inequality and destructive forces. Capitalism's death drive drives society and humans into death. Its necropolitical tendencies lead to deaths through wars, genocide and crime; the death of nature through pollution and human-made disasters; the death of democracy in fascism and authoritarianism; the death of truth in ideology; the death of self-management and self-control through exploitation and class rule; the death of humanity through classist, gendered, racist and fascist violence; etc.

In capitalism, death has become a taboo. Because death is a capitalist reality, we tend to try to mentally escape it, which is why it is rendered a taboo topic that humans avoid talking about. As a consequence, there is also the illusion that there is nothing common in the way humans encounter death in different parts of the world. Because we do not talk about death, we do not know what common experiences of and encounters with death we humans have and make.

We try to constantly replace the old and the dying by the new in order to forget about death. We try to make death disappear by consumer culture, commodification, new technologies, fast food culture, McDonaldisation, acceleration, the information flood, the beauty industry, the cult of youth, care homes where the old and the ill disappear, celebrity culture, the online influencer culture of likes and selfies, cosmetic surgeries, fashion, brands, individualised mourning/suffering/dying/crying, techniques of rendering killings in wars invisible, cyborg utopias that are actual dystopias, etc. We thereby try to turn death into a 'disappearing act' (Bauman 1992, 172) without realising how real and permanently present death is within capitalism and how it is killing humanity.

Immortality has become an industry and a constant labour that wants to create 'private vehicles to eternity' (Bauman, in: Jacobsen and Kearl 2014, 314). Capitalist modernity and individualism have brought about the 'sequestration of sickness and death', their 'concealment from general view', so that death has become a 'technical matter' (Giddens 1991, 161) removed from everyday life and put into the hands of medical and care institutions and professionals. Death as taboo means we do not talk about death, dying and the dead. The incommunicability of death is part of death's big capitalist disappearing act. As a consequence, we do not know what common experiences, assessments and preferences of death humans have. But there are empirical studies conducted in different societies that help us gain insights into universal aspects of dying.

COVID-19 had antagonistic effects on the visibility of death. On the one hand, COVID-19 deaths were talked about constantly in the public sphere – in the media and in private conversations, which made death visible to the public. On the other hand, the actual processes of death due to infection risks disappeared behind closed hospital doors, which further advanced the sequestration and invisibility of death that had step by step and bit by bit started to become reversed with the rise of, for example, death cafés, online forums dedicated to illnesses and deaths, communication about deceased individuals on social media, public discussions about assisted suicide, virtual cemeteries, online memorials, etc. (Pentaris and Woodthorpe 2022; Walter, Hourizi, Moncur and Pitsillides 2011). Based on these insights, the next section focuses on the role of communication in dying.

3. COMMUNICATION'S ROLE IN THE QUALITY OF LIFE AND DYING

3.1 A Look at Some Empirical Studies

Let us have a brief and exemplary overview look at what some empirical studies have found out about how humans think about death.

A significant amount of relevant studies has been carried out in Western countries. Sandsdalen et al. (2015) systematically compared 25 studies that analysed patients' preferences in palliative care. There were seven studies from the UK, five from the US, four from Canada and one each from Australia, Finland, Hong Kong, Ireland, Israel, Italy, Japan, the Netherlands and New Zealand. The total number of patients participating in these studies was 1,583. The studies were published between 1982 and 2012.

> *The focus on living involved being with people whom patients loved and enjoyed. Family and friends were the main source of support and strength by being there for patients, reassuring them and having a history of managing hard times together. Patients therefore preferred facilitation of companionship and care by family and friends and opportunities to maintain and strengthen important relationships. [...] Patients expressed preferences for personnel who communicated with them by spending time listening to their concerns, using an interactive dialogue and contributing to being understood.*
>
> (Sandsdalen et al. 2015, 411, 413)

Steinhauser et al. (2000) conducted a survey in the US, in which 340 seriously ill patients, 332 members of recently bereaved families, 361 physicians and 429 care providers participated. Among the statements that achieved a very high level of agreement among all four groups of participants were that it was important for a dying person to have 'someone who will listen', say 'goodbye to important people', to be able to 'discuss fears' with a physician, resolve 'unfinished business with family or friends', have 'physical touch', share 'time with close friends', '[p]resence of family', to '[n]ot die alone', to have a nurse 'with whom one feels comfortable', to know that one's physician is 'comfortable talking about death and dying', and to have a physician who knows one as a 'whole person' (Steinhauser et al. 2000, 2479). Out of 26 aspects of high agreement, 12 aspects were communicative and social in character, which shows the importance of communication in dying.

Studies carried out in Asian societies found results comparable to the ones created by studies in Western societies. For example, Hou et al. (2019) conducted a survey among 248

Chinese advanced cancer patients about aspects of a good death. They found that 'the "good relationship with family" had the highest score. China is a family-centred country and a dying person needs his or her family members to provide care, financial and emotional support; thus, a good relationship with family is essential for patients. [...] saying what he or she want to dear people before breathing the last breath in the GDI is something of great importance' (Hou et al. 2019, 5).

Miyashita et al. (2007) developed the Good Death Inventory, a questionnaire that consists of 18 components of a good death. They conducted a national survey where 2,548 Japanese participated. It showed that besides physical and psychological comfort and caring physicians and nurses, social contact with the family to whom one can express one's feelings and whose support one gets was a key aspect of a good death. Miyashita et al. (2007, 1094) stress that Western studies made similar findings and that there are elements of a good death that transcend cultural differences.

Pitanupong and Janmanee (2021) conducted a survey among 96 palliative cancer patients in Thailand. Of the respondents surveyed, 93.8% said it is important to have 'loved ones around when needed' (2021, 4).

Studies of dying in African societies created insights comparable to the ones from Asian and Western societies. A study of 173 terminally ill Ugandan patients showed that the vast majority preferred to be cared for at home. The patients said that at home, 'I feel safe and I am surrounded by my family' (Kikule 2003, 193). Namisango, Katabira, Karamagi and Baguma (2007) studied the quality of life perceptions among 200 advanced AIDS patients in Uganda. They found that interpersonal relations, including the ability to talk about important things to close people and spending as much time as one wants to with friends and family, achieved the highest score in the respondents' assessment of what constitutes good quality of life.

Selman et al. (2011) conducted a quality of life survey among 285 palliative care patients in Uganda and South Africa. It showed that having close personal relations was the most important quality of life for the respondents. Using a five-point Likert scale (1 = low importance, 5 = very high importance), the average answer score to the question 'It is important to me to have close personal relationships' was 4.13.

3.2 Theoretical Interpretation: The Universality of Communication From the Cradle to the Grave

These studies of human assessments of dying from different parts of the world provide empirical insights that indicate that humans across cultures and beyond cultural differences have common social features when it comes to dying and death. According to the presented studies, humans wish to die without pain and suffering, at an old age after a fulfilled and happy life, and in close contact with their loved ones.

It seems to be a universal feature of humans that when being very ill or dying, they want to be surrounded by and spend time with family and friends, want to console loved ones and be consoled by them, long for human closeness and touch and want to have caring physicians and nurses who take time to speak with them and treat them humanely. Humans are social beings from the cradle to the grave. We are born as social beings, we live as social beings and we die as social beings. As infants, toddlers and children we, just like when we are ill and die, need other humans who are there for us and care for us. Caring and being cared for is an essential feature of what it means to be human. Love is an essential and common feature of human behaviour. We have to love and be loved in order to lead fulfilled lives. We live our lives in and through social relations. Close social relations, love, family and friendships are of particular importance for human development. Communication is the process of the production and reproduction of social relations (Fuchs 2020a). To be human not just means to be a social being. It also means to be a communicative being. The social is communicative. And communication is social. Dying and the death of loved ones are existential situations where we directly experience the temporal, physical and social limits of human existence. Communicating with loved ones, feeling their love, holding their hands and looking into their faces are of key importance to humans in such existential situations.

Death is endstrangement, estrangement and alienation without end (Fuchs 2020a, 322–325): the ultimate alienation from ourselves; the ultimate alienation from our loved ones; the ultimate alienation from society; the ultimate alienation from self-consciousness, the body and the mind; the ultimate alienation from the world and the ultimate alienation from communication (social death). In the passage to death, in the process of dying, humans face ultimate alienation, their endstrangement, which is the ultimate unknown. Coping with this ultimate unknown in light of their own end, humans desire to be close to what they know and what they are most familiar with – their loved ones. This is why communication with loved ones, physical proximity, feeling and communicating love, are so important for the dying human person.

The importance that humans give to communication and sociality when dying shows that communication and sociality are human, cultural and social universals. Empirical studies of dying confirm the insights of philosophers such as Kwasi Wiredu and Jürgen Habermas.

Kwasi Wiredu (1995) opposes cultural relativism and argues that there are cultural universals, features of all societies and all humans in all societies. Humans have in common that they 'go beyond instinct' by 'means of reflective perception, abstraction, deduction, and indication' (53). Reflective perception means 'a kind of awareness that involves the identification of objects and events through the conscious application of concepts and which entails, consequently, the power of recall and re-identification' (53). Before acting, humans anticipate consequences of possible actions, which are based on their power of judgement and their power of inference (53). 'Action, then, involves judgment and inference, but social action, an essential ingredient of human existence, involves, besides these, communication. Now, if a being is capable of judgment and inference, then, necessarily, it is capable of communication' (54). The 'possession of one language or another by all human societies [...] is the cultural universal *par excellence*' (59). 'No human society or community is possible without communication' (Wiredu 1996, 13); humans are born with 'innate conceptual abilities' (Wiredu 1996, 19), the capacities to develop language and to communicate.

Jürgen Habermas has advanced an approach comparable to Wiredu's. Habermas is critical of postmodern thought's relativism that denies there are universals. 'Repulsion towards the One and veneration of difference and the Other obscures the dialectical connection between them. [...] The unity of reason is still treated as repression, not as the source of the diversity of its voice' (Habermas 1992, 140). The capitalist and bureaucratic colonisation of the lifeworld is for Habermas the cause of postmodernism's loss of focus on unity (Habermas 1992, 140–141). Habermas defends the idea of the unity of human activity arguing that the unity of reason lies in the diversity of human voices. Through communication, humans produce and realise their unity.

> *[C]oncepts like truth, rationality, or justification play the same grammatical role in every linguistic community. Certainly, some cultures have had more practice than others at distancing themselves from themselves. But all languages offer the possibility of distinguishing between what is true and what we hold to be true. The supposition of a common objective world is built into the pragmatics of every single linguistic usage. And the dialogue roles of every speech situation enforce a symmetry in participant perspectives*
>
> (Habermas 1992, 138).

Without communication there is no society, so communication is certainly a universal feature of all societies. This is just another way of saying that social relations are the key feature of all societies. But social relations are not just cultural in character; they exist in all social systems, which makes them foundational. Social relations are the medium and outcome of communication processes. Communication is the production and reproduction of social relations in society (Fuchs 2020a). Therefore, social production is at the heart of all human activity and societies. Social production means the production of social forms in and through humans that encounter each other in various ways. There are not just cultural universal but social universals of societies, which means that humans are social and societal beings. And for being social, they have to produce and communicate. For producing, humans utilise communication. And communication is a production process. Communication is (a type of) production; production is (also) communication. Anticipatory thinking, what Wiredu calls reflective perception, is part of human production, as Marx (1867, 284) knew:

> *But what distinguishes the worst architect from the best of bees is that the architect builds the cell in his mind be-fore he constructs it in wax. At the end of*

> *every labour process, a result emerges which had already been conceived by the worker at the beginning, hence already existed ideally. Man not only effects a change of form in the materials of nature; he also realizes* [verwirklicht] *his own purpose in those materials. And this is a purpose he is conscious of.*

Communication is a human, social and societal universal. We communicate and need social relations as soon as we are born, communicate all our lives and have a desire for communication when the time comes that we are dying. Communication is a universal human need, want and desire from the cradle to the grave. It is a human universal.

Studies found there is a relatively high incongruence between the preferred and the actual place of death (Bell, Emese and Masaki 2010, Fischer et al. 2013). In 2019, 56.5 million humans died; 17.4% of them were aged below 40; 11.0% of those who died were less than 20 years old; 4.3 million (7.6%) died from injuries that would have been avoidable such as transport injuries (2.3%) and unintentional injuries (falls, drowning, fire, carbon monoxide, etc.); around 500,000 (around 1%) died from interpersonal violence, conflict, wars and terrorism; and 2.3 million (around 4%) died from work-related accidents or diseases.[1–2] Oxfam (2021) estimates that 11 humans die every minute from acute hunger, which is almost 16,000 per day and 5.78 million per year. This means that around 10% of all deaths are the consequence of starvation.

---

1 Data source for all data presented in this paragraph (if not indicated otherwise): Global Health Data Exchange, data for the year 2019, http://ghdx.healthdata.org/gbd-results-tool, accessed on 24 July 2021.

2 Data source: https://www.ilo.org/moscow/areas-of-work/occupational-safety-and-health/WCMS_249278/lang–en/index.htm, accessed on 24 July 2021.

The presented data show that a significant number and share of humans die other than they wish to. For example, they die at an early age, as a consequence of accidents, labour and class relations, hunger, or violence. We live in a capitalist world system. Given that a significant number of deaths are avoidable and the result of social consequences such as inequalities, poverty, political conflict and class relations, it is evident that capitalism kills. Capitalism is a deadly system.

Political economy affects death and the quality of life and dying. Capitalism's severe inequality has resulted in hunger. In 2020, more than 800 million humans were malnourished, 98% of them lived in developing countries (Mercy Corps 2020). Patients in poor countries often face a lack of access to pain relief, hospitals, treatment, palliative care, lack of and high morbidity and mortality among medical personnel (Harding and Higginson 2005). During the COVID-19 pandemic, lack of medical resources such as oxygen in poor countries such as India resulted in many people suffocating to death. Researchers estimate that between March 2020 and June 2021, the number of excess deaths in India was between 3.4 and 4.9 million (Anand, Sandefur and Subramanian 2021).

There is a difference between how humans want to die and how they actually die. The reality is that many humans do not die in ways they see as a good death, but they die a bad death. Death is always horrible, tragic and beyond words. The terms 'good death', 'quality of death', 'quality of dying' and 'good dying' that are used in medical science are therefore not really appropriate. Death and dying are inherently negative and bad. Nobody wants to lose loved ones. But there is a difference between living a long, fulfilled, loving life without pain and dying because of war, genocide, sexual violence, murder, hunger, curable diseases or at a young age.

This section engaged with empirical studies that show that humans wish to die in company and in a social and communicative manner, which corresponds to fundamental universal human characteristics. Humans' ideal of dying often diverges from the reality of dying (Broad et al. 2013, Fischer et al. 2013). Capitalism's destructive character worsens this divergence. In the next section, we will analyse the role of communication in the context of dying in the COVID-19 pandemic.

4. DYING AND COMMUNICATION IN THE COVID-19 PANDEMIC

Dying in the COVID-19 pandemic was horrible for both the ill person and their relatives and friends. When hospitals were overcrowded, humans died at home or on the streets from COVID-19. Their relatives or friends in such cases were with them, so they were not alone, but many of them suffocated to death, which means a cruel death. Others made it into hospitals and intensive care units, where they had to be isolated from family and friends, who were not allowed to visit them in order to minimise the infection risk.

As the previous section of this essay shows, we know from empirical studies that humans prefer to die in company and communication with their loved ones. Dying from COVID-19 in a hospital is brutal because the wish of humans to die in company with close friends remains unrealised. The horrors of COVID-19 include that the direct social link between hospitalised patients and their loved ones is broken, there is no close company by loved ones when patients experience the fear of dying and doctors tell them that they have to be intubated and ventilated, that many patients do not have direct contact and do not feel the touch of their loved ones and vice-versa, that patients experience a de-personalised form of treatment because doctors and nurses have to wear protective equipment and that many family members and friends are not able to once more see the deceased loved one and cannot properly plan and attend the funeral. Death is always horrible. Dying from COVID-19 is particularly inhumane because the inherent human need for communication and company with loved ones is broken. COVID-19 is therefore a particularly horrible disease.

In the COVID-19 pandemic, masks, gloves, phones, tablets, software and apps mediated and shaped the quality of the communication between patients and loved ones and the communication between patients and their families and health care personnel. Digital technologies played an important role in the communication of illness and death in the COVID-19 pandemic.

There have been some empirical studies of communicative aspects of suffering from and dying from COVID-19 (e.g. Bear et al. 2020, Burrell and Selman 2020, Chen, Lerman and Ferrara 2020, Ersek et al. 2021, Feder et al. 2021, Hanna et al. 2021a, 2021b, Kürtüncü, Kurt and Arslan 2021, Mortazavi et al. 2021, Selman et al. 2021). Methods used have included surveys, semi-structured interviews and analysis of Twitter data. Research participants have included survivors of the illness, family members, health care professionals, faith communities, non-religious civil society groups and vulnerable groups.

4.1 Dying From COVID-19

Empirical studies show how dreadful hospitalised COVID-19 patients, especially those in intensive care units, found not being able to in person see their loved ones in the hospital and in the moment of dying. The same is true for funerals.

Hospitalised COVID-19 patients described their situation in the following ways: 'I felt completely alone'; 'I was going mad' (Kürtüncü, Kurt and Arslan 2021, 7). Bereaved family members characterised this situation, for example, in the following words:

> *Dad died alone. My world stopped when he died. He was my hero.*
>
> (Selman et al. 2021, 1271)

> *Why couldn't I go in to see him? I feel hurt. I can't do anything to bring him back.*
>
> (Feder et al. 2021, 589)

> *I wished before he went on the ventilator that I would have liked to speak to him more than that one time.*
>
> (Feder et al. 2021, 590)

> *when he died, I took the grave-clothes to shroud him, but they didn't allow me*
>
> (Mortazavi et al. 2021, 9).

> *I was up against the window as close as I could get. He was talking to me which I could hear but he couldn't hear me back, so it became distressing for both of us*
>
> (Hanna et al. 2021a, 847).

> *The actual fact that we could go there and see her, because we hadn't seen her for so long. It was important being able to touch her one last time and talk to her*
>
> (Hanna et al. 2021a, 848).

The policies and practices of close family members being able or not able to in person meet dying COVID-19 patients and attending their funerals varied from country to country and from institution to institution. In quite some cases, there was a complete ban of family members entering hospitals and care homes, whereas in others single family members were allowed to be present when their loved ones died.

No matter if loved ones are briefly present or not present at all when COVID-19 patients die, the situation is horrible. There is not enough privacy, not enough time for communication and not enough physical closeness. Dying and death are always inhumane. Dying and being buried without or with very little contact to your loved ones are not just inhumane, but barbaric and a horror version of dying and death. I am in no way saying that hospitals and care homes should have allowed anyone in all the time. There were real infection risks. Rather, I stress what horrific and brutal ways of death this pandemic called forth. Dying from COVID-19 in many cases completely destroyed the social and communicative nature of human beings, denying them essential human contact with loved ones when they died. COVID-19 has not just killed millions of humans but killed them in barbaric manners.

Interviews with health care professionals who provided end of life care of COVID-19 patients showed the difficulty many such professionals faced because of the high number of patients and the lack of staff caused by the illness and death of colleagues who had caught the virus (Hanna et al. 2021b, 1252). In cases where a patient died alone, health care professionals had the difficult task of informing relatives, which they often found more difficult due the lack of opportunity for building relationships to the patients' families: 'Many professionals were concerned about whether a relative would have other people around to provide comfort when they received this call. At times, health and social care professionals working in hospital settings felt it was challenging to share this news with relatives, as they had not had an opportunity to develop a rapport or relationship with them, having never met physically or virtually' (Hanna et al. 2021b, 1253).

Even if close relatives were allowed to be present when their loved one died from COVID-19, some of them faced unbridgeable hurdles having to do with spatial distance and their own health: 'Health and social care professionals stated that visiting restrictions at end of life meant that usually only one relative could spend time with the dying family member as death became imminent, presenting families with a difficult choice. [...] A number of relatives were unable to spend time with their dying family member at end of life because they were "shielding", or lived too far away. In the absence of visiting, some professionals felt it was important to ask relatives if and how the healthcare team could facilitate the spiritual and emotional needs of the patient and family when death was imminent' (Hanna et al. 2021b, 1254, 1255).

Language skills were another source of anxiety: 'Fears of a loved one dying alone are especially amplified amongst diaspora populations who worry that elderly loved ones, who may not speak fluent English, will not even be able to communicate with hospital staff. Fears of a "bad death" are also amplified in communities that have historically experienced traumatic forms of death and burial, or if the deceased is young' (Bear et al. 2020, 15).

Many health care professionals feel that flexible visiting arrangements at the end of the life of COVID-19 patients are important: 'Due to the unpredictability of when a death may happen, recognition of the importance of flexible visiting arrangements at end of life in light of pandemic-related restrictions may reduce tension within clinical teams, and avoid health and social care professionals feeling they have to "*break the rules*" in order to deliver optimal family-centred care'. (Hanna et al. 2021b, 1255).

Fifty-eight interviews in the UK across religious communities showed that many such communities find dying in company important: 'Across communities, a "good death" in these challenging circumstances means allowing the deceased to die with company (ideally that of loved ones, or someone who can provide spiritual support), ensuring their body undergoes appropriate ritual procedures (even if the ritual has been modified for the pandemic), and respecting their wishes regarding burial or cremation' (Bear et al. 2020, 15).

4.2 Digital Communication and Dying in the COVID-19 Pandemic

Digital information and communication technologies played an important role in the mediation of dying, funerals and mourning in the COVID-19 pandemic.

Family members of COVID-19 patients argue that staying in touch with their loved ones via video apps was important:

> *Facetime should be mandatory if the family wants it – it made all the difference*
>
> (Feder et al. 2021, 590)

> *He couldn't talk. It was extraordinary of the staff to call me every day.*
>
> (Feder et al. 2021, 589)

> *'The last time we saw him he was unconscious,' a family member reported, 'the nurse FaceTimed us when he woke up. That was very special'.*
>
> (Feder et al. 2021, 590)

> *Characteristics of perceived high-quality communication included staff availability for remote communication and being kept informed of the patient's condition and plan of care. Low-quality communication with staff was perceived to result from limited access to staff, insufficient updates regarding the patient's condition, and when the family member was not consulted about care decision-making.*
>
> (Feder et al. 2021, 587)

> *Some health and social care professionals felt video calls enabled a sense of connectedness between the patient and their usual family life; [...] Other health and social care professionals reported that video calls were rarely offered or facilitated because professionals or families feared it could be too distressing for either the patient or relative.*
>
> (Hanna et al. 2021b, 1254)

Having digitally mediated contact to seriously ill or dying COVID-19 patients is certainly preferable for both the patients and their loved ones than having no contact at all. But the digital mediation of dying should not be celebrated and idealised, but rather be seen as an aspect of the horrors of COVID-19. Mobile phones, tables, apps, video chat, text and audio messages, etc. cannot replace direct human contact and the longing for physical touch, love and direct human presence that dying individuals and their loved ones have. Seriously ill and dying COVID-19 patients and their loved ones long for communication, love, physical touch and physical proximity. Digitally mediated communication involves spatial distance, sometimes – as in the case of audio messages – also temporal distance, which is why it cannot compensate for, replace or simulate the quality of physical co-presence of seriously ill humans and their loved ones. You cannot look your loved ones in the eyes via a video app. You cannot feel your loved ones' hands and bodies via an app. You cannot smell them on WhatsApp. You cannot wipe their tears via a tablet. You cannot caress your loved ones online. You cannot kiss them when there is digital mediation. The digital mediation of death and dying is part of the brutality and horror of dying. In the situation of serious illness, digital communication is for many humans preferable to no communicate at all, but it is still a form of alienated dying, an alienation from how humans want to die. Once labour, leisure, friendships, family, sexuality, life, dying, 'worshipping and organizing funerals begins to take place solely across the interface of screens, it is time to acknowledge that on all sides we are surrounded by rings of fire. To a great extent, the digital is the new gaping hole exploding Earth' (Mbembe 2021, S60). Digital mediation, acceleration and superficiality have become everyday aspects of social relations. These processes therefore also shaped the horrors of death and death communication in the COVID-19 pandemic.

When someone dies, their body and mind die and with them, there is social death, social relations and communication cease. What some people characterise as a 'good death' includes the simultaneous physical and social death of an individual, which means that their communicative links to loved ones remain until the end. Part of the horror of deaths in the COVID-19 pandemic is the socio-temporal distancing of social death and physical death. The direct communicative ties to loved ones are cut before physical death sets in. At best, there is digital communication, which might however fail and cannot properly communicate love.

Further problems in the digital mediation of dying and illness are the digital skills gap that affects especially older and less educated individuals; instances where there is the lack of access to mobile phones, tablets and laptops; the lack of time of health care professionals to adequately support patients in digital communication; or the lack of reliable and fast internet connections in hospitals and care homes which makes connections patchy and digital communication incomprehensible. Neoliberal assaults on public services, privatisation, austerity measures and global inequalities have starved many health care systems' resources. As a consequence, there often is not enough time, money, personnel and technology for organising the digital mediation of sickness and dying. Digital divides and inequalities affect the quality of illness and dying. COVID-19 patients who were digitally disadvantaged were more likely to die lonely, which negates and violates the communicative and social nature of human beings.

In empirical studies, bereaved family members reported about such problems:

> *He had no idea how to use Zoom and no one helped him. iPad wasn't offered. So inadequate for hospice patient.*
>
> (Feder et al. 2021, 590)

> *No one ever offered me any video, or FaceTiming with my father. My father died without ever seeing me or me seeing my father for the last time.*
>
> (Feder et al. 2021, 590)

> *Looking back, it was easier to have these conversations face to face as the family are usually there and you can provide a bit more emotional support*
>
> (Hanna et al. 2021b, 1253)

> *It was four days before he died, and I said to Mum 'why don't you ask the nurses if they can put the phone to his ear and you can say the things you want to'. So, she did and the nurse on the telephone basically said, 'there's no point in doing that [I'm] sure he won't be able to hear you', which we both were quite upset by.*
>
> (Hanna et al. 2021a, 848)

Some humans experienced the digital mediation of funerals and mourning positively, while others as alienating:

> *My uncle died of COVID-19 on Monday. It kills us he died alone! We aren't able to physically be together. But thank you [videoconferencing provider] for creating a virtual platform where we were able to have a vigil & continue our traditional Novena-9 days of Rosary to pray for him as a family.*
>
> (Selman et al. 2021, 1272)

> *...virtual space really helped us a lot during this time. [...] we did not gather for the sake of our children and we saw each other virtually through telecommunications.*
>
> (Mortazavi et al. 2021, 12)

> *...they used live video on Instagram to allow the others to attend the funeral virtually. [...] it was unreal.*
>
> (Mortazavi et al. 2021, 10)

Digitally mediated funerals are better than lonely funerals that nobody attends. But they are not proper replacements, compensations or substitutions for the quality of family members, friends, fellows and colleagues coming together in person at the funeral of a deceased person. The labour of mourning is a particularly negative, sad and alienating type of labour. Mourning is in contemporary societies often individualised. Death and the suffering caused by death are taboos in individualised societies. Funerals where humans meet in person and socially organise and share the labour of mourning are opportunities to cut through and transcend individualism, which is part of giving solace. Mediated participation in a funeral is not the same as participation in person. It is better that such opportunities exist than that they do not exist so that friends who live far away can participate. But completely virtual funerals, where individuals sitting alone at home watch how the coffin of their loved one is buried, how the deceased is cremated or how a robot disperses the deceased's ash into a lake or the sea are absolutely alienated funerals. Digitally automated, digitally mediated and digitally distanced funerals create social distance in situations where closeness, direct social contact, proximity and community are needed.

In the next section, we will generalise the insights from Sections 3 and 4 with the help of the notion of capitalist necropower. This requires that we take the broader societal picture of death into account, which allows us to develop the notion of capitalist necropower.

5. CAPITALIST NECROPOWER IN COVID-CAPITALISM

5.1 What Is Capitalist Necropower?

The political theorist and philosopher Achille Mbembe coined the notions of necropower and necropolitics. Necropolitics and necropower mean 'forms of subjugation of life to the power of death', the creation of '*death-worlds*' where deadly living conditions are created and the subjugation of humans to 'living conditions that confer upon them the status of the *living dead*' (Mbembe 2019, 92). Mbembe points towards capitalism's deadly and destructive potentials. But he goes too far in his analysis that often presents modernity as such as colonial and necropolitical. For example, Mbembe argues that Marx's 'commitment to the abolition of commodity production' and the 'overcoming of class divisions' disrespect 'human plurality' and has to result in 'a fight to the death' as well as in '[t]error and killing' (Mbembe 2019, 74).

Stalinism and its versions certainly have been forms of organised terror that, however, did not aim at abolishing class but to create a state-capitalist system with new class relations. Class relations are not an aspect of 'human plurality' but rather the creation of conditions where some lead a good life at the expense of others whom they exploit. Marx's goal was a true form of individuality and plurality through creation of common conditions of ownership of the means of production, social justice and socio-technological development so that everyone can fully enjoy and engage in the plurality and possibilities of life. For Marx, there is an alternative, democratic-socialist modernity that enables all humans to lead a good life. Socialism for Marx enables 'the richest development of the individuals' (1857/1958, 541), and 'time for the full development of the individual' (1857/1858, 711) and 'makes it possible for me to do one thing today and another tomorrow' (Marx and Engels 1845/1846, 47). The plurality that Mbembe calls for cannot be realised through class relations but through democratic socialism that strengthens what Marx terms 'rich individuality which is all-sided' (Marx 1857/1858, 325).

The notions of necropolitics and necropower are helpful when put into the context of capitalist society. It is important to stress the political economy of necropower more strongly than Mbembe does, which means to foreground that capitalism creates destructive forces. Capitalism is based on a dialectic of production and destruction. Capitalism is a necrophilic, death-bringing, death-producing, destructive system. Its productive forces and social relations turn into destructive forces and deadly forces. That capitalism, that is capitalist societies and capitalist world society, is necrophilic and necrotic means that deadly and destructive forces operate in this system on the levels and through the interaction of economy, politics and ideology. Necropower is therefore not, as in Foucaultian perspectives, simply political, but political-economic. Necropower is in the contemporary world system capitalist necropower. Talking about necropower means that we have to talk about capitalism. Class relations, that is, exploitation and domination are the sources of destruction and death in contemporary societies and the world system. Class and domination are at the heart of the capitalist system, that is, a formation of society (or what Marx terms 'Gesellschaftsformation') that is based on the accumulation of capital and power through exploitation of labour and the domination of human activities.

Comparable to Mbembe, the sociologist and philosopher Erich Fromm analysed the role of death in society. Whereas Mbembe's main starting points and influences have been Michel Foucault and Frantz Fanon, Fromm bases his analysis on Karl Marx and Sigmund Freud.

Freud (1961, 1990, 1962) argues that the human structure of instincts consists in the interplay of the life instincts (Eros), which 'seeks to force together and hold together the portions of living substance' and aim at advancing love (Freud 1961, 55), and the death instincts that aim at advancing 'aggressiveness and destructiveness' (Freud 1962, 66). There is no doubt that humans in contemporary societies love and kill, but the question is if the implication is that humans have an innate death drive.

Whereas for Freud, human aggressiveness, destructiveness and narcissism are biologically given, constant and unchangeable in nature, for Fromm, these human capacities are socially developed, historical and changeable. Fromm characterises the role of life and death in humanity in the following manner:

> *I believe that man's basic alternative is the choice between life and death. Every act implies this choice. Man is free to make it, but this freedom is a limited one. There are many favorable and unfavorable conditions which incline him – his psychological constitution, the condition of the specific society into which he was born, his family, teachers, and the friends he meets and chooses. It is man's task to enlarge the margin of freedom, to strengthen the conditions which are conducive to life as against those which are conducive to death. Life and death, as spoken of here, are not the biological states, but states of being, of relating to the world. Life means constant change, constant birth. Death means cessation of growth, ossification, repetition. The unhappy fate of many is that they do not make the choice. They are neither alive nor dead. Life becomes a burden, an aimless enterprise, and busyness is the means to protect one from the torture of being in the land of shadows*
>
> (Fromm 1962/2009, 134)

For Fromm, the death drive does not exist as human essence but is immanent in authoritarian and capitalist societies. Not the human being, but capitalism has a death drive. 'Capitalism is based on the principle that is to be found in all class societies: the use of man by man' (Fromm 1956/2002, 90). In a society that is based on exploitation and domination, 'the will to destroy must rise when the will to create cannot be satisfied' (Fromm 1956/2002, 36). Capitalism 'transforms all life into things' (Fromm 1973/1997, 350) so that the 'world becomes a sum of lifeless artifacts' (Fromm 1973/1997, 350). The outcome is that capitalism has the potentials to create a 'world of death and decay' (Fromm 1973/1997, 351).

Capitalism creates what Fromm terms necrophilia, the desire and tendency of dominant classes and groups to artificially create death. Necrophilia is an intensification of sadism that takes on new qualities (Fromm 1973/1997, 463). Necrophilia is not a medical disease, but what Fromm (1965c) terms a social character. Society's political economy, its class and economic structure, the education system, dominant forms of socialisation and upbringing, religion, traditions, etc. shape the social character. Necrophilia is a feature of behaviour that can be found as a result of authoritarian socialisation patterns and in authoritarian, fascist and capitalist societies. Societies, groups and individuals shaped by the necrophilic social character have '*the* passion to destroy life and the attraction to all that is dead, decaying, and purely mechanical' (Fromm 1973/1997, 6); they love the 'act of dismemberment' (329), 'to destroy for the sake of destruction' (186) and 'to tear apart living structures' (329). Necrophilic societies, groups and individuals have 'the passion to transform that which is alive into something un-alive; to destroy for the sake of destruction' (Fromm 1973/1997, 332).

The consequences of necrophilic societies are death, exclusion, the exploitation of humans and the destruction of the world: 'The world of life has become a world of "no-life"; persons have become "nonpersons", a world of death. [...] Man, in the name of progress, is transforming the world into a stinking and poisonous place (and this is *not* symbolic). He pollutes the air, the water, the soil, the animals-and himself' (Fromm 1973/1997, 350).

Banerjee (2008) speaks of necrocapitalism as the 'practices of organizational accumulation that involve violence, dispossession, and death' (1543), 'torture, suicide, slavery, destruction of livelihoods, and the general management of violence' (1548) and the denial of access to resources that are essential to humans' 'health and life' (1551). Banerjee's approach is important in that it points out the deadly and violent dimension of capitalism.

Other than Agamben (2005), who sees the creation of states of exception as opportunities for raw violence, I argue that in capitalism, states of exception are the rule. Capitalism is not a form of necropower that creates death and destruction only in specific phases such as war. Capitalism is inherently necrophilic, destructive and death-producing. 'Necrocapitalism' is a tautology and misnomer. The term can easily be understood as implying that death and destruction are limited to specific moments, events or phases in capitalist development. In contrast, I use the term 'capitalist necropower' for maintaining that necrophilia and the death drive are immanent to capitalism and that capitalism requires rule by force, has destructive effects and accumulates capital and power through destroying life and opportunities for self-management.

Capitalism does not only create 'blood and fire' (Marx 1867, 875) in its initial or exceptional phases, but rather blood, dirt and fire are constituents and results of capitalist accumulation processes. Capitalism creates by destroying, which results in death, blood, dirt, fire and waste. Capitalism not just creates things and commodities that are dead labour, but it also produces dead bodies, dead minds and dead species. Enmity is immanent to capitalism. Capitalism produces by destroying, which results in the 'waste of the workers' life and health' (Marx 1894, 182). Capitalism 'squanders human beings, living labour, more readily than does any other mode of production, squandering not only flesh and blood, but nerves and brains as well' (Marx 1894, 182).

The difference between capitalist society and democratic socialism is the one between death/life, destruction/construction, having/being, hatred/love, competition/co-operation, egoism/solidarity, exploitation/commoning, private property/common property of the means of production, dictatorship/democracy, ideology/friendship, violence/kindness, racism and patriarchy/undivided humanity, war, imperialism and colonialism/peaceful life together, fetishism/social life, wage labour and slavery/free activity under conditions of wealth for all, instrumental reason/cooperative reason, etc.

The history of capitalism is also a history of destruction and violence, which means a history of the societal death drive – a history of wars, slave trade, nationalism, fascism, racist violence, sexual violence, terrorism and genocide. Violence has been one of the means that have been employed for exploiting labour and exerting political control. It has an economic and a political dimension. But violence also has an ideological dimension. Ideology creates friends and enemies, insiders and outsiders, in order to stir hatred against the constructed enemies and deflect attention from class rule and how society's problems are grounded in dominant powers. Ideology breeds violence. Capitalism's victims of violence have always been confronted with the brutality of death and were robbed of the possibility of a good death.

Horkheimer and Adorno speak of the dialectic of the enlightenment as capitalism's potential to turn instrumental rationality into irrationality and 'steer society toward barbarism' (2002, 15). Nazi-fascism has created a singular form of terror – it industrially organised the suffocation of millions of Jews in gas chambers. Fascism is death as politically organised terror. Auschwitz is the symbol of how instrumental reason has the potential to result in the industrial organisation of death in the form of barbarism. 'In the camps death has a novel horror; since Auschwitz, fearing death means fearing worse than death' (Adorno 1973/2004, 371). Anti-semitism is older than capitalism, but has played an important ideological role in capitalism. 'Modern anti-Semitism [...] is a particularly pernicious fetish form.. [...] [The] specific characteristics of the power attributed to the Jews by modern anti-Semitism – abstractness, intangibility, universality, mobility – are all characteristics of the value dimension of the social forms fundamentally characterizing capitalism' (Postone 2003, 95, 91). Nazi-fascism claimed there was an unproductive, parasitic 'Jewish' sphere of circulation and finance on the one side, and a productive 'Aryan' sphere of industrial capital on the other. Moishe Postone argues that modern anti-semitism is a biologisation and naturalisation of the commodity fetish. The ideological friend/enemy distinction set-up thereby resulted in the Nazi system's barbarism of industrial mass murder of millions of Jews.

Racism has in the form of colonial violence, slavery and the exploitation and discrimination of people of colour played an important role in capitalism. The police murder of George Floyd is a symbol of how the potentials of racist violence are ever-present in capitalist societies. He was murdered in a barbaric manner by a policeman who cut off his ability to breathe. Capitalism has denied humans air – the right to breathe and the right to life. Racial capitalism has suffocated and strangled people of colour to death in numerous manners. Imperialist capitalism has caused the last breath of innumerable humans in wars of conquest. Colonial capitalism has created slaves without rights whose breath can be chocked anytime by slave masters without facing legal consequences.

Fascism and racism operate with the dualisms of nature and society that are ideologically turned into friend/enemy distinctions where one side is presented as by biological or cultural nature superior and the other side as inferior. Nature in capitalism not only plays an ideological role but is also used as a means and object of production. Fossil capitalism has polluted the air and destroyed parts of nature, which has caused the death of countless human beings and species. Capitalism has appropriated nature in destructive manners. Capitalism's drive for destruction manifests itself in 'simultaneously undermining the original sources of all wealth – the soil and the worker' (Marx 1867, 638). Capitalism's relations and forces are 'destructive forces' (Marx and Engels 1845/1846, 439), which speaks for the creation of a new 'association of individuals on the basis created by modern productive forces and world intercourse' (Marx and Engels 1845/1846, 439).

5.2 Capitalist Necropower in the Age of COVID-19

Capitalism is not the direct cause but a context of the COVID-19 pandemic that has unleashed a new dimension of necropower throughout societies and the capitalist world system. Agricultural capitalism has destroyed biodiversity and increased the chance of zoonotic spillovers of deadly viruses from animals to humans so that deadly pandemics caused by a virus such as SARS-CoV-2, which have robbed hundreds of millions of humans their breath and have killed so many of them, became more likely (Davis 2020, Foster and Suwandi 2020, Fuchs 2021a, chapter 1, Wallace 2020). The global activities of capitalist agribusinesses and their expropriation of cheap land have destroyed natural habitat, have had negative impacts on humans, animal species and plants, and created the foundations of SARS-CoV-2. The result has been the loss of biodiversity, which has brought wild animals such as bats into closer contact with humans and has in turn increased the chance of the spillover of dangerous viruses from animals to humans. Bats carry many pathogens. Capitalist deforestation and urbanisation have brought bats and other wild animals into closer contact with humans. Eating wild animals has become fashionable among parts of the new bourgeoisie, has turned pangolins, lemurs, bats, racoons, squirrels, rats, badgers, etc., into luxury commodities and has created the job of wild animal hunters as wage labour.

The COVID-19 pandemic is a manifestation of the current world system's destructive forces. Capitalism's inequalities have been reproduced in COVID-19 capitalism. Members of groups such as the poor who cannot afford and are not able to socially distance and work from home, workers in key industries, health care workers, the urban poor living in cramped ghettos, migrant workers and people of colour who disproportionately have low-paid jobs in the personal service and blue-collar sector where social distancing is not possible, and others have disproportionately died from COVID-19. During the pandemic, digital technologies helped to keep society and social relations going. When it comes to death and dying, digital technologies mediating the last contact with loved ones and funerals without direct contact, physical proximity and human touch are an expression and manifestation of the coldness and brutality of COVID-capitalism.

In countries, where governments advanced social Darwinist policies that put the economy over humans lives and were based on the principle of the survival of the fittest, there were COVID-19 surplus deaths, that is, an excess of deaths that would have been preventable and avoidable if proper protective measures had been implemented in a timely manner. Given the complexity of the COVID-19 pandemic and that vaccines against and treatment of a new deadly virus are not readily available, a certain number of deaths is to be expected in a pandemic. Experts, however, also know how to minimise deaths, which includes the recommendation to widely shut down public life. Politicians who disregarded this advice did not take the pandemic seriously and advanced COVID necropolitics, a politics that created surplus deaths and tolerated such surpluses.

Conducting mathematical analysis of COVID-19 data for 32 countries, Dergiades, Milas, Mossialos and Panagiotidis (2020, 4) found that 'the greater the strength of government interventions at an early stage, the more effective these are in slowing down or reversing the growth rate of deaths'. Conversely, this means that countries where governments implemented lax or no lockdown measures, there tended to be a high number of deaths. The authors used the Oxford Government Stringency Index, a composite indicator that measures the strength of government responses to COVID-19 at single points of time using nine variables, namely 'school closures; workplace closures; cancellation of public events; restrictions on public gatherings; closures of public transport; stay-at-home requirements; public information campaigns; restrictions on internal movements and international travel controls'.[3]

COVID-19 necropoliticians considered keeping the economy open more important than saving human lives. 'It is not a coincidence that the calls to open the economy were uttered after it became clear that marginalized communities are the one's suffering most during this crisis. [...] The poor, working class, and those within communities of color were expendable' (Fletcher and Waraschinski 2022, 216, 210).

The US, India, Brazil, Russia and the UK are among the countries with the highest total number of COVID deaths. Between the start of the pandemic and 25 July 2021, according

3 https://ourworldindata.org/policy-responses-covid, accessed on 25 July 2021.

to official data, 604,546 humans died from COVID-19 in the US, 419,470 in India, 545,604 in Brazil and 128,980 in the UK.[4] The governments of these countries in general took rather lax lockdown measures. It is not a surprise that countries with authoritarian, right-wing governments that resisted lockdowns or implemented them half-heartedly or very late tended to have large numbers of COVID deaths.

In the US, Donald Trump took relatively lax measures against the spread of COVID-19. He also played down how severe and dangerous the virus was. On 9 March 2020, he tweeted: 'So last year 37,000 Americans died from the common Flu. It averages between 27,000 and 70,000 per year. Nothing is shut down, life & the economy go on. At this moment there are 546 confirmed cases of CoronaVirus, with 22 deaths. Think about that!'.[5]

In India, President Narendra Modi allowed the Kumbh Mela festival to proceed in April 2021, where millions of Indians participated without social distancing and masks. On 14 April, around a million people took a holy bath in the River Ganges without social distancing. In late April, there were more than 400,000 daily new COVID-19 cases in India. On April 30, there were 402,014 reported cases (Slater and Masih 2021).

Indian public intellectual Arundhati Roy (2021) commented:

> *There was also the Kumbh Mela to be organised, so that millions of Hindu pilgrims could crowd together in a small town to bathe in the Ganges and spread the virus even-handedly as they returned to their homes across the country, blessed and purified. […]*

---

4 Data source: WHO, https://covid19.who.int/table, accessed on 25 July 2021.

5 Data source: http://web.archive.org/web/20200309145720/.

People are dying in hospital corridors, on roads and in their homes. Crematoriums in Delhi have run out of firewood. The forest department has had to give special permission for the felling of city trees. Desperate people are using whatever kindling they can find. Parks and car parks are being turned into cremation grounds. […] The [health care] system has not collapsed. The 'system' barely existed. The government – this one, as well as the Congress government that preceded it – deliberately dismantled what little medical infrastructure there was. This is what happens when a pandemic hits a country with an almost nonexistent public healthcare system. […] This massive privatisation of India's healthcare is a crime. The system hasn't collapsed. The government has failed. […] what we are witnessing is […] an outright crime against humanity.

While several hundred thousand of Brazilians died from COVID-19, Brazil's president Jair Bolsonaro said about the disease:

Now everything is about the pandemic. […] we will all die one day, everyone here will die. It is no use running away from it, running away from reality. This must stop being a country of sissies

(Mussato 2020)

For 90% of the population, this will be a little flu or nothing.

(France24, 2021)

> *masks are harmful for children, causing irritability, headache, concentration difficulties, a reduction in feelings of happiness*
>
> (France24, 2021)

In a parliamentary enquiry, Boris Johnson's former Chief Adviser Dominic Cummings described the approach to COVID-19 of the British prime minister and his government:

> *His [Boris Johnson's] argument then was, 'We shouldn't have done the first lockdown, and I am not going to make the same mistake again'. [...] the Prime Minister took the view in January/February that economic harm caused by action against Covid was going to be more damaging to the country than Covid itself. We could not persuade him that if you basically took the view, 'Let it rip, and don't worry about Covid', you would not just get all the health disasters but also a huge economic disaster.*
>
> (Health and Social Care Committee and Science and Technology Committee 2021)

In a BBC interview, Cummings said Johnson wanted to let COVID-19 'wash through the country' because people dying from it were 'essentially all over 80' and Johnson did 'no longer buy all this NHS overwhelmed stuff' (BBC 2021). In late June 2021, Sajid Javid became UK Secretary of State for Health and Social Care. On 19 July, the UK lifted virtually all COVID-related restrictions of public life, a decision on which Johnson and Javid had major influence. Javid tweeted that 'we learn to live with, rather than cower from, this virus'.[6]

6 Data source: https://web.archive.org/web/20210725055847if_/https://twitter.com/sajidjavid/status/1418932718847541248, accessed on 26 July 2021.

'Learning to live' with COVID means accepting that humans die from the virus and suffer from long COVID as a consequence of a lack of protective measures.

The world's necropoliticians are predominantly right-wing. In the COVID-19 pandemic, their actions made more humans die than was necessary because they put economic interests over human interests and believe in the necrophilic principle of the survival of the fittest in society; they brought health care systems close to collapse by letting infection numbers explode; by doing so, they risked the development of new virus variants and more deaths; they especially put ill and old people and disadvantaged groups at an increased risk of dying; they were responsible for surplus deaths and that many people experienced a lonely death in isolation where there was no last contact with loved ones or such contact took place only at a distance via digital technologies that lack the possibility for human touch. Necropoliticians are anti-Humanists. Guided by the necrophilic ideology that conceives society in terms of egoism, competition, warfare and survival of the fittest, their (non-)management of the COVID-19 pandemic intensified and extended the deadly power of the pandemic.

6. CONCLUSION

This essay asked: What is the role of the communication of death and dying in capitalist society? How has communication with dying loved ones changed in the COVID-19 pandemic? What roles have digital technologies and capitalism played in this context?

We can now summarise the main findings:

- In capitalist societies, death and dying are taboo topics and are hidden, invisible and institutionalised. The COVID-19 pandemic had contradictory effects on the role of death in society. While on the one hand death became a public, constantly talked-about topic that dominated the public sphere, humans dying from COVID-19 were isolated and often died alone hidden from others and without contact to their loved ones, which advanced the sequestration of sickness and death.

- Empirical studies show that humans wish to die in company and in a social and communicative manner, which corresponds to fundamental universal human characteristics. The analysed studies confirm the insights of the philosophers Kwasi Wiredu and Jürgen Habermas that humans are fundamentally social and communicative beings from the cradle to the grave. This is why humans want to die in company with their loved ones. The ideal of dying often diverges from the reality of dying. Capitalism's destructive character worsens this divergence.
- COVID-19 in many cases destroyed the social and communicative nature of human beings, denying them essential human contact with loved ones when they died.
- Digital information and communication technologies played an important role in the mediation of dying, funerals and mourning in the COVID-19 pandemic.
- Empirical studies show that seriously ill and dying COVID-19 patients and their loved ones long for communication, love, physical touch and physical proximity. Part of the horror of deaths in the COVID-19 pandemic is the spatio-temporal distancing of social death and physical death. The direct communicative ties to loved ones are cut before physical death sets in. At best, there is digital communication, which might however fail and cannot properly communicate love. The digital mediation of dying

should not be celebrated and idealised, but rather be seen as an aspect of the horrors of COVID-19. Mobile phones, tables, apps, video chat, text and audio messages, etc. cannot replace direct human contact and the longing for physical touch, love and direct human presence that dying individuals and their loved ones have.

- Necropower is the power to advance death and destruction. Necropower is not, as in a Foucaultian perspective, simply political. And it is also not, as for Freud, simply psychological and individual. Necropower is political-economic. Capitalist necropower means that capitalism is a necrophilic, death-bringing, death-producing, destructive system. The history of capitalism is also a history of destruction and violence. Capitalism is not the direct cause but a context of the COVID-19 pandemic that has unleashed a new dimension of necropower throughout societies and the capitalist world system. Necropoliticians based their responses to the COVID-19 pandemic on the necrophilic principle of the survival of the fittest, which intensified and extended the deadly power of the pandemic. They were responsible for surplus deaths and that many people experienced a lonely death in isolation where there was no last contact with loved ones or such contact took place only at a distance via digital technologies that lack the possibility for human touch.

There are alternatives to necropower and capitalism's death drive that causes devastation and exploitation. Capitalist necropower is not naturally given, but a historical fact, which means it can be undone by social struggle. Already today there are 'antinecrophilous tendencies' and developments (Fromm 1973/1997, 358), struggles for solidarity, equality, justice and freedom for all. Fromm argues that capitalism's death drive can be overcome 'by our reassertion of our bond to life, by a response to the love of others that may kindle our own love' (Fromm 1979, 127), which requires the creation of a democratic socialist society (see the contributions in Fromm 1965b).

Humans require love in order to exist. They do not require authoritarianism, hatred and destruction to exist. That is why love and solidarity are foundational to human existence, while destruction and competition are not. Humans as such are biophilic beings. 'Biophilia is the passionate love of life and of all that is alive; it is the wish to further growth, whether in a person, a plant, an idea, or a social group. The biophilous person prefers to construct rather than to retain. He is capable of wondering, and he prefers to see something new rather than to find confirmation of the old. He loves the adventure of living more than he does certainty. He sees the whole rather than only the parts, structures rather than summations. He wants to mold and to influence by love, reason, and example' (Fromm 1973/1997, 365). 'Love of life or' love of the dead is the fundamental alternative' (Fromm 1973/1997, 366). Capitalism has advanced the forces of death that have found a new culmination in COVID-19 capitalism.

The authoritarian and necrophilic social character destroys, exploits, dictates and manipulates. The Humanist social character loves, creates, practices democracy and friendship. Whereas class societies are based on the principles of exploitation, dictatorship and ideology, democratic socialism is based on the principles of sharing and the commons, participatory democracy and friendship (see Table 7.1, based on Fuchs 2020a, 103). Class societies are based on necrophilia, and democratic socialism is based on love as societal principle.

Socialist society is a society shaped by biophilia and Humanism, which means that it enables a good life and advantages for all. Democratic socialism means to 'replace manipulation of men by active and intelligent co-operation,

Table 7.1. Principles of Class Societies and Democratic Socialism.

Realm of Society	Class and Authoritarian Societies	Democratic Socialism
Economy	Exploitation	Sharing the commons
Politics	Dictatorship	Participatory democracy
Culture	Ideology	Friendship

and expand the principle of government of the people, by the people, for the people, from the formal political to the economic sphere' (Fromm 1965a, 300). Fromm cites the philosopher Paul Tillich, saying that democratic socialism is 'a resistance movement against the destruction of love in social reality' (Tillich 1952, 6; cited in Fromm 2004, 49). Democratic socialism replaces death by love. In democratic socialism, humans will continue to die, but they will lead better and more fulfilled lives than in class societies. There is the chance that in democratic socialist societies, death loses its horrors when all humans know and can be assured that what they leave behind is a good society and a good life for their loved ones. Natural and social disasters, maybe also pandemics, will continue to exist in democratic socialism, but they will become more unlikely and society will be better prepared to manage them. In addition, there will not be necrophilic politicians who act irresponsibly and intensify the horrors of death.

8

CONCLUSION

1. FOR RADICAL HUMANISM AND RADICAL DIGITAL HUMANISM

Enlightenment Humanism promised freedom, equality and solidarity for all. Capitalism's reality is that it subverts the Enlightenment and results in outbursts of irrationality and 'antireason' that unleashed destructive forces that can result in 'the extermination of humanity' (Horkheimer and Adorno 2002, 43). This book has argued that in light of the global problems humanity faces, we should not abandon the Enlightenment and humanism, but fully realise them so that all humans benefit. The 'wounds which enlightenment has left behind' are 'the moments where enlightenment itself betrays its own imperfect character and reveals that it is actually not yet enlightened enough. And it is only by pursuing the principle of enlightenment through to the end that these wounds may perhaps be healed' (Adorno 2017, 188). Digital Humanism is a theory and praxis of how to heal the deep wounds of the Enlightenment that capitalism created.

Humanity is in a crisis. Digital capitalism and digital authoritarianism have brought society to the verge of collapse.

We face the danger of the rise of new fascisms, global war, the descent into barbarism and the extinction of life on Earth. This book asked: Why is Humanist philosophy important in the contemporary digital age? How can Humanism help us to critically understand how digital technologies shape society and humanity? What kind of Humanism do we need to make sense of digitalisation in society? It introduced the approach of Digital Humanism and showed how a radical version of Humanism allows us to critically analyse the roles of digital technologies in society.

Humanism is a philosophical approach that stresses the active and transformative capacities of human beings in the social world. Digital Humanism is a philosophical approach that stresses the active and transformative capacities of human beings in the digital age. Radical/Socialist Humanism is a materialist philosophy that stresses the productive, social and transformative capacities of human beings that enable them to liberate themselves from class society, capitalism, exploitation, domination, and ideology and to together create a better world. Radical Digital Humanism is a materialist approach to the study of, reflection on, and development of digital technologies and digital society that is focused on the need of humans to liberate themselves from digital class society, digital capitalism, digital exploitation, digital domination, and digital ideology and to together create a good digital society. Radical Digital Humanism stands in the tradition of both Humanism and Radical Humanism. It is Radical Humanism in and for the digital age.

Radical Humanism argues for the decolonisation of universities and academia. First and foremost, this means that it challenges university capitalism and neoliberalism. University capitalism and the corporate, instrumental university have been the result of neo-colonialism. Academic decolonisation means challenge the unequal political economy that underpins knowledge production in global capitalism. The true decolonisation of academia has to include weakening the logic of capitalism in this realm of society. The decolonisation of academia includes the commonification, democratisation and self-management of academia. Decolonisation is not a moral question and not a question of individual behaviour, but first and foremost a question of political economy and power. To decolonise the university means to transform university capitalism into public-interest and commons-oriented universities that advance the public good and a good society. It means to challenge neo-colonialism.

Radical Digital Humanism is critical of conservatism, authoritarianism, post-structuralism, Post-humanism, Transhumanism, technological determinism, accelerationism and the social construction of technology. Digital technologies such as Artificial Intelligence (AI) and robots do not have certain automatic impacts on society. Class antagonisms, power struggles, class struggles shape the development, use, and impacts of digital and other technologies in capitalist society. Radical Humanism helps creating and sustaining technologies for the many, not the few. Radical Digital Humanism rejects the idea to replace humans by or transform them into digital machines. Rather, it sees digital machines as possibilities that as part of struggles for a society that benefits all humans can expand, help realising and more fully develop the potentials of humans and society.

Humans wish to die in company and in a social and communicative manner, which corresponds to fundamental universal human characteristics. COVID-19 in many cases destroyed the social and communicative nature of human beings, denying them essential human contact with loved ones when they died. Part of the horror of deaths in the COVID-19 pandemic is the spatio-temporal distancing of social death and physical death. Necropower is the power to advance death and destruction. Capitalist necropower means that capitalism is a necrophilic, death-bringing, death-producing, destructive system. The history of capitalism is also a history of destruction and violence. Necropoliticians based their responses to the COVID-19 pandemic on the necrophilic principle of the survival of the fittest, which intensified and extended the deadly power of the pandemic. Natural and social disasters, maybe also pandemics, will continue to exist in democratic socialism, but they will become more unlikely and society will be better prepared to manage them. In addition, there will not be necrophilic politicians who act irresponsibly and intensify the horrors of death.

2. SOCIALISM OR BARBARISM, HUMANISM OR AUTHORITARIANISM, DEMOCRACY OR FASCISM

Rosa Luxemburg was one of the twentieth century's major Radical Humanists. She analysed how capitalism produced inequalities, war, destruction and misery. She opposed the idea that the alternative to capitalism is dictatorship and argued that democratic socialism is the alternative to capitalism and authoritarianism. She was a radical analyst, public intellectual, political leader and activist. Just like at the time of Rosa Luxemburg, society is at a crossroads today. Humanity faces the choice between democracy and fascism, socialism and barbarism, Humanism and authoritarianism. Once again, '[b]ourgeois society stands at the crossroads, either transition to socialism or regression into barbarism' (Luxemburg 1916, 388). 'In this hour, socialism is the only salvation for humanity' (Luxemburg 1971, 367). In order to guarantee that there will be a future for humans, society and nature, we need Radical Humanism.

Radical Humanism is not simply a vision of democratic socialism but also class and social struggles. For doing so, specific demands and intermediate goals of struggle are needed. Such demands emerge from radical humanists coming together and organising themselves collectively. Radical Humanism wants to improve the living conditions of those who are exploited and oppressed already in the here and now.

3. WE NEED TO PROPERLY TAX CAPITAL AND STRENGTHEN WORKING CLASS INTERESTS

One important aspect of Radical Humanism is the strengthening of labour in the class relation to capital. This includes the struggle for wage increases, the abolishment of precarious labour, the reduction of the working week with full wage compensation etc. One important measure is to tax capital properly, especially transnational corporations. For decades, giant corporations operating globally have made lots of profits and achieved high profit rates by exploiting labour and paying no or little taxes. Globalisation of their financial operations has allowed them to escape from and avoid taxation. And legislation and nation-states enabled them to do so. As a consequence of the COVID-19 pandemic and after Joe Biden became US President in 2021, more talks and plans emerged to increase capital taxation. In 2021, the OECD and the G20 reached a global agreement on corporate taxation. They agreed a minimum tax rate of 15% on large transnational corporations' profits. This level is lower than the national corporation tax level of many countries. Workers pay significantly higher taxes on their wages than this minimum level. Given transnational corporations have for decades paid very little in corporation tax, which has made their owners richer and richer, a minimum corporation tax rate, double of what was agreed (30%), is feasible. The tax income should be used to build and expand welfare states and public services. It is in this context important that an agreed share goes to poor countries and benefits the world's poor.

Another important realm where urgent political transformations are needed is the public sphere where information and news are produced, circulated and consumed in public where humans engage in political discourse. The public sphere has been dominated by ideology, monopoly media corporations, state control, surveillance, 'fake news', post-truth culture, algorithmic politics, high speed flows of superficial news, filter bubbles, echo chambers, fragmented public spheres that are isolated, the friend/enemy scheme that has led to a radical polarisation and the spread of hatred that is often expressed online, and new forms of nationalism, authoritarianism and fascism. The public sphere is so polarised that groups with different opinions do not rationally debate. They ignore each other. They hate each other. There are online threats. There is violence. There is a pathway towards a global war. Will this pathway be stopped? How can it be stopped?

There are no easy answers and no easy solutions. One element of stopping violence and circumventing war is to deescalate conflicts and make those with opposing views talk to each other. In international politics, this is called diplomacy. In everyday political life, we need more reasonable political debate. And we need a proper infrastructure for political debate. Commercial media and capitalist Internet platforms fail in providing platforms for reasonable political debate. Their profit logic stands in contradiction to communicative action in the public sphere. Not-for-profit media are better at creating and providing high-quality platforms for news and debate.

4. WE NEED A PUBLIC SERVICE INTERNET

Public Service Media (PSM) play an important role in advancing a humanist public sphere. PSM are media of the public, by the public, and for the public. They are publicly funded and not oriented on profit and capital accumulation. They are funded by the public and engage the public. They advance the public sphere by the distinct PSM remit that commits them to provide services that provide high-quality information, news, education, entertainment and communication so that PSM support the development of democracy, culture and citizenship. PSM have faced attacks on their existence and independence. Capitalist and authoritarian forces like to either control PSM or do away with them. Proper PSM that deserve this name and fully realise the principles of PSM do not exist everywhere. PSM help to advance Humanism in society. They should therefore not be rolled back, cut or abolished but supported, advanced, intensified and extended. Twenty-first century democracy needs PSM. The twenty-first century public sphere needs PSM. Twenty-first century Humanism needs PSM. The PSM and Public Service Internet Manifesto is a call and demand to safeguard the existence, independence and funding of PSM and to create a Public Service Internet (Public Service Media and Public Service Internet Manifesto 2021, see also Fuchs and Unterberger 2021). The Manifesto is an expression and application of Humanism in the realm of media, communication, culture and the public sphere. It says:

> *A democracy-enhancing Internet requires Public Service Media becoming Public Service Internet platforms that help to advance opportunities and equality in society. We call for the creation of the legal, economic and organisational foundations of*

such platforms. [...] The digital giants have weakened democracy and the Internet. We need a new Internet. We need to rebuild the Internet. While the contemporary Internet is dominated by monopolies and commerce, the Public Service Internet is dominated by democracy. While the contemporary Internet is dominated by surveillance, the Public Service Internet is privacy-friendly and transparent. While the contemporary Internet misinforms and separates the public, the Public Service Internet engages, informs and supports the public. While the contemporary Internet is driven by and drives the profit principle, the Public Service Internet puts social needs first.

(Public Service Media and Public Service Internet Manifesto 2021)

Users of the Internet and social media in contemporary capitalism face 10 problems (see Fuchs 2021c, especially chapter 15):

1. *Digital capital* exploits *digital labour*. It creates *corporate digital monopolies* and precarious life.
2. *Digital individualism* is focused on the accumulation of attention for and agreement to individual social media profiles and postings. It treats humans as mere competitors and enemies, which undermines human solidarity.
3. The state and corporations conduct *digital surveillance* in the surveillance-industrial Internet complex.
4. Social media are *unsocial, anti-social social media*. Edward Snowden's revelations and the Cambridge Analytica scandal show that capitalist social media pose threat to

democracy. Ideologues and demagogues spread *digital authoritarianism* on social media.

5. Automated, *algorithmic politics* dominates social media. Automated computer programmes ('bots') replace human activities, post information and create 'likes'. It has become more difficult to identify if information and dis/agreements stem from humans or machines.
6. There are *fragmented online publics* dominated by filter bubbles.
7. The *digital culture industry* has created *digital ideology* and social media as *digital tabloids* and giant corporate digital monopolies. Online advertising and tabloid entertainment dominate over and displace political and educational content.
8. On social media, *influencer capitalism* creates asymmetries of attention, visibility and a commodity culture that promotes an online world of non-stop shopping.
9. *Digital acceleration* exceeds our attention capacities with superficial information flows processed at very high speed on social media. There is a lack of online time and space for conversations and debates on social media.
10. There are *post-factual politics and false news* on social media. In the age of new nationalisms and new authoritarianism, a culture has emerged that results in the publication and spread of false online news, the distrust of facts and the emotionalisation of politics.

Renewing public service media and creating a public service Internet is needed for saving democracy and the public sphere.

The important message that needs to be repeated publicly as often as possible is the following one: PSM are key for securing the democratic public sphere. Their funding and independence need to be secured for upholding democracy. The problems caused by corporate Internet platforms and the lack of alternatives are strong arguments in favour of securing the existence of PSM and extending their remit, resources and funding in the light of the digital age.

A public and commons-based Internet is possible – an Internet on which people share, communicate, decide, discuss, play, create, criticise, network, collaborate, find, maintain and build friendships, fall in love, entertain themselves and each other, educate themselves as common activity without corporate mediation.

Public service Internet platforms are provided by PSM organisations with a not-for-profit imperative and the digital remit to advance information, news, debate, democracy, education, entertainment, participation and creativity with the help of the Internet.

PSM should redefine their remit as the digital remit to advance information, entertainment, education and democracy by utilising digital platforms.

For advancing public service Internet platforms, we need funding and resources, digital remit of public service media, new ideas for platforms and formats, development projects, and research projects.

But for achieving a sustainable, inclusive, diverse, humane, democratic, fair and just digital society, more is needed. We need to properly tax (digital) capital in the form of an advertising tax, a digital services tax, a licence fee paid by companies and an increase of corporation tax.

We require the improvement of the working conditions in the digital and cultural industries, leading to the abolishment of precarious labour.

The monopolies of the digital giants should be ended via anti-trust laws, socialisation and commonification.

We need privacy-friendly data protection laws, opt-in policies to targeted/digital advertising, the proper regulation of political and targeted online advertising, the support and advancement of corporate watch platforms, fact-checking organisations/platforms, platform co-operatives and slow media.

And we need new, innovative, creative ideas for new platforms and formats as well as their realisation. Examples are a public service YouTube operated by an international network of PSM that make available their archive material by the use of Creative Commons CC-BY-NC licences and support user participation and user-generated content production in new ways (Fuchs 2021, 374–375). The lack of public debate culture should be overcome by new formats and platforms that build on the Club 2/After Dark format of uncensored, open-ended live debate updated to the digital age so that there is some level of user participation via an online platform (Fuchs 2021, 375–379). I call this concept Club 2.0 (Fuchs 2021, 375–379).

A different media world is possible. A Public Service Internet and revitalised PSM are urgently needed for sustaining democracy!

5. WE NEED RADICAL HUMANISM

The PSM and Public Service Internet Manifesto makes the point that we need to safeguard the existence, funding and independence of PSM and that these media's public service remit should be expanded into a digital remit. While PSM are under attack by authoritarian and populist governments, parties and movements, we need to advance the ideas of the Manifesto as a counterpoint. That's why everyone should sign the Manifesto, spread its ideas, and ask others to join and support this initiative.

The proper taxation of capital, including digital capital, in order to extend and intensify welfare states, eradicate poverty and advancing socio-economic inequality as well as the creation of a public service Internet are just two of the policy measures a Radical Humanism of the twenty-first century should strive to advance. There are many more realms of society that those committed to Humanism must look at and many more measures they should struggle for. Concrete campaigns, demands and policies emerge from political organisation and struggles. Radical Humanism is an urgent project for the twenty-first century. Facing the danger of the extinction of the nature, society, and humanity and the descendance into barbarism, we need Radical Humanism now. We need Radical Humanism as philosophy of praxis and political project. We do not know how the world will look in 20, 50 and a 100 years from now. We do know that without Radical Humanist praxis society might collapse. Radical Humanism is the antidote to destruction, exploitation, oppression, fascism and barbarism. Radical Humanism is the most urgent task for the twenty-first century.

BIBLIOGRAPHY

Adorno, Theodor W. 2019. *Ontology and Dialectics*. Cambridge: Polity.

Adorno, Theodor W. 2017. *An Introduction to Dialectics*. Cambridge: Polity.

Adorno, Theodor W. 2006. *History and Freedom: Lectures 1964–1965*. Cambridge: Polity.

Adorno, Theodor W. 1973/2004. *Negative Dialectics*. London: Routledge.

Agamben, Giorgio. 2005. *The State of Exception*. Chicago: The University of Chicago Press.

Alderson, David, and Robert Spencer, eds. 2017. *For Humanism. Explorations in Theory and Politics*. London: Pluto.

All on Robots. 2021. "Types of Robots". June 16. https://www.allonrobots.com/types-of-robots/.

Amin, Samir. 1980. *Class and Nation, Historically and in the Current Crisis*. London: Heinemann.

Anand, Abhishek, Justin Sandefur, and Arvind Subramanian. 2021. *Three New Estimates of India's All-Cause Excess Mortality during the COVID-19 Pandemic*. Center for Global

Development Working Paper 589. Washington: Center for Global Development.

Andrews, John. 2010. *The Book of Isms*. London: Profile.

Aristotle. 2002. *Nicomachean Ethics*. Translated by Joe Sachs. Indianapolis: Hackett.

Asante, Molefi Kete, and Clyde E. Ledbetter, eds. 2016. *Contemporary Critical Thought in Africology and Africana Studies*. Lanham: Lexington Books.

Balibar, Étienne, and Immanuel Wallerstein. 1991. *Race, Nation, Class. Ambiguous Identities*. London: Verso.

Banerjee, Subhabrata Bobby. 2008. "Necrocapitalism". *Organization Studies* 29 (12): 1541–1563.

Bastani, Aaron. 2019. *Fully Automated Luxury Communism*. London: Verso.

Bauman, Zygmunt. 1992. *Mortality, Immortality and Other Life Strategies*. Cambridge: Polity.

BBC. 2021. "Covid: Boris Johnson Resisted Autumn Lockdown as Only Over-80s Dying – Dominic Cummings". *BBC*, July 20. https://www.bbc.com/news/uk-politics-57854811.

Bear, Laura et al. 2020. "'A Good Death' during the Covid-19 Pandemic in the UK: A Report on Key Findings and Recommendations". http://eprints.lse.ac.uk/104143.

Begum, Neema, and Rima Saini. 2019. "Decolonising the Curriculum". *Political Studies Review* 17 (2): 196–201.

Bell, Christina L., Emese Somogyi-Zalud, and Kamal H. Masaki. 2010. "Factors Associated with Congruence between Preferred and Actual Place of Death". *Journal of Pain and Symptom Management* 39 (3): 591–604.

Bhambra, Gurminder K., Dalia Gebrial, and Kerem Nişancıoğlu, eds. 2018. *Decolonising the University*. London: Pluto.

Blaut, James Morris. 1989. "Colonialism and the Rise of Capitalism". *Science & Society* 53 (3): 260–296.

Boden, Margaret A. 2018. *Artificial Intelligence: A Very Short Introduction*. Oxford: Oxford University Press.

Broad, Joanna B., Merryn Gott, Hongsoo Kim, Michal Boyd, He Chen, and Martin J. Connolly. 2013. "Where Do People Die? An International Comparison of the Percentage of Deaths Occurring in Hospital and Residential Care Settings in 45 Populations, Using Published and Available Statistics". *International Journal of Public Health* 58 (2): 257–267.

Burrell, Alexander, and Lucy E. Selman. 2020. "How do Funeral Practices Impact Bereaved Relatives' Mental Health, Grief and Bereavement? A Mixed Methods Review with Implications for COVID-19". *Omega: The Journal of Death and Dying*. doi:10.1177/0030222820941296.

Chakravartty, Paula, Rachel Kuo, Victoria Grubbs, and Charlton McIlwain. 2018. "#CommunicationSoWhite". *Journal of Communication* 68 (2): 254–266.

Chatterjee, Satischandra, and Dhirendramohan Datta. 2007. *An Introduction to Indian Philosophy*. New Delhi: Rupa.

Chen, Emily, Kristina Lerman, and Emilio Ferrara. 2020. "Tracking Social Media Discourse about the COVID-19 Pandemic: Development of a Public Coronavirus Twitter Data Set". *JMIR Public Health and Surveillance* 6 (2): e19273. doi: 10.2196/19273.

Clynes, Manfred E., and Nathan S. Kline. 1960/1995. "Cyborgs and Space". In *The Cyborg Handbook*, 29–34. New York: Routledge.

Copson, Andrew. 2015. "What Is Humanism?" In *The Wiley Blackwell Handbook of Humanism*, edited by Andrew Copson, and A. C. Grayling, 1–33. Chicester: Wiley Blackwell.

Curran, James, and Myung-Jin Park, eds. 2000. *De-Westernizing Media Studies*. London: Routledge.

Davis, Mike. 2020. *The Monster Enters: COVID-19, Avian Flu and the Plagues of Capitalism*. New York: OR Books.

Digital Humanism Initiative. 2019. "Vienna Manifesto on Digital Humanism". Accessed August 5, 2021. https://dighum.ec.tuwien.ac.at/dighum-manifesto.

Dreyfus, Hubert. 1986. *Mind Over Machine. The Power of Human Intuition and Expertise in the Era of the Computer*. New York: Free Press.

Dutta, Mohan J. 2020. "Whiteness, Internationalization, and Erasure: Decolonizing Futures from the Global South". *Communication and Critical/Cultural Studies* 17 (2): 228–235.

Ersek, Mary et al. 2021. "End-of-Life Care in the Time of COVID-19: Communication Matters More than Ever". *Journal of Pain and Symptom Management* 62 (2): 213–222.

Ertel, Wolfgang. 2017. *Introduction to Artificial Intelligence*, 2nd ed. London: Springer.

Escobar, Arturo. 2018. *Designs for the Pluriverse. Radical Interdependence, Autonomy, and the Making of Worlds*. Durham: Duke University Press.

European Commission. 2018. "Artificial Intelligence in Europe". Accessed June 22, 2021. https://eur-lex.europa.eu/legal-content/EN/TXT/?uri=COM%3A2018%3A237%3AFIN.

Fanon, Frantz. 1963. *The Wretched of the Earth*. New York: Grove Press.

Feder, Shelli et al. 2021. "'Why Couldn't I Go in to See Him?' Bereaved Families' Perceptions of End-of-Life Communication during COVID-19". *Journal of the American Geriatrics Society* 69 (3): 587–592.

Fischer, Stacy et al. 2013. "Where Do You Want to Spend Your Last Days of Life? Low Concordance between Preferred and Actual Site of Death among Hospitalized Adults". *Journal of Hospital Medicine* 8 (4): 178–183.

Fletcher, Kami, and Tamara Waraschinski. 2022. "Between Cultural Necrophilia and African American Activism: Life and Loss in the Age of COVID". In *Death, Grief and Loss in the Context of COVID-19*, edited by Panagiotis Pentaris, 209–228. London: Routledge.

Flisfeder, Matthew, and Clint Burnham. 2017. "Love and Sex in the Age of Capitalist Realism: On Spike Jonze's Her". *Cinema Journal* 57 (1): 25–45.

Foster, John Bellamy, and Intan Suwandi. 2020. "COVID-19 and Catastrophe Capitalism". *Monthly Review* 72 (2). https://monthlyreview.org/2020/06/01/covid-19-and-catastrophe-capitalism/.

Fowler, Jeaneane. 2015. "The Materialists of Classical India". In *The Wiley Blackwell Handbook of Humanism*, edited by Andrew Copson, and A. C. Grayling, 97–118. Chicester: Wiley Blackwell.

Fowler, Merv. 2015. "Ancient China". In *The Wiley Blackwell Handbook of Humanism*, edited by Andrew Copson, and A. C. Grayling, 133–152. Chicester: Wiley Blackwell.

France24. 2021. "Bolsonaro's Most Controversial Coronavirus Quotes". France24, 19 June 2021. https://www.france24.com/en/live-news/20210619-bolsonaro-s-most-controversial-coronavirus-quotes.

Freeman, Charles. 2015. "Humanism in the Classical World". In *The Wiley Blackwell Handbook of Humanism*, edited by Andrew Copson, and A. C. Grayling, 119–132. Chicester: Wiley Blackwell.

Frente de Libertação de Moçambique (FRELIMO). 1965/1982. "Colonialism and Neo-Colonialism". In *The African Liberation Reader: Documents of the National Liberation Movements. Volume 1: The Anatomy of Colonialism*, edited by Aquino de Bragança, and Immanuel Wallerstein, 3–5. London: Zed.

Freud, Sigmund. 1990. *The Ego and the Id*. New York: W. W. Norton & do not die what.

Freud, Sigmund. 1962. *Civilization and Its Discontents*. New York: W. W. Norton & Company.

Freud, Sigmund. 1961. *Beyond the Pleasure Principle*. New York: W. W. Norton & Company.

Freud, Sigmund. 1918. "Our Attitude towards Death". In *The Standard Edition of the Complete Psychological Works of Sigmund Freud: Volume XIV*, edited by James Strachey, 289–300. London: The Hogarth Press.

Fromm, Erich. 2004. *Marx's Concept of Man*. London: Continuum.

Fromm, Erich. 1979. *To Have or to Be*. London: Sphere Books.

Fromm, Erich. 1976/1997. *To Have or to Be?* London: Continuum.

Fromm, Erich. 1973/1997. *The Anatomy of Human Destructiveness*. London: Pimlico.

Fromm, Erich. 1966. *You Shall be as Gods*. New York: Fawcett Premier.

Fromm, Erich. 1965a. *Escape from Freedom*. New York: Avon.

Fromm, Erich, ed. 1965b. *Socialist Humanism. An International Symposium*. Garden City: Doubleday & Company.

Fromm, Erich. 1965c. "The Application of Humanist Psychoanalysis to Marx's Theory". In *Socialist Humanism: An International Symposium*, edited by Erich Fromm, 207–222. Garden City: Doubleday.

Fromm, Erich. 1962/2009. *Beyond the Chains of Illusion: My Encounter with Marx and Freud*. New York: Continuum.

Fromm, Erich. 1961/2003. *Marx's Concept of Man*. London: Continuum.

Fromm, Erich. 1956/2002. *The Sane Society*. London: Routledge.

Fromm, Erich. 1947/2003. *Man for Himself: An Inquiry into the Psychology of Ethics*. Abingdon: Routledge.

Fuchs, Christian. 2021a. *Communicating COVID-19. Everyday Life, Digital Capitalism, and Conspiracy Theories in Pandemic Times*. Bingley: Emerald Publishing Limited.

Fuchs, Christian. 2021b. "Foundations of Communication/ Media/Digital (In)Justice". *Journal of Media Ethics* (forthcoming, accepted for publication).

Fuchs, Christian. 2021c. *Social Media: A Critical Introduction*, 3rd ed. London: Sage.

Fuchs, Christian. 2020a. *Communication and Capitalism: A Critical Theory*. London: University of Westminster Press. doi:10.16997/book45.

Fuchs, Christian, ed. 2020b. "Communicative Socialism/ Digital Socialism". *tripleC: Communication, Capitalism & Critique* 18 (1): 1–285. doi:10.31269/triplec.v18i1.1149.

Fuchs, Christian. 2020c. *Marxism: Karl Marx's Fifteen Key Concepts for Cultural & Communication Studies*. New York: Routledge.

Fuchs, Christian. 2018. *Digital Demagogue: Authoritarian Capitalism in the Age of Trump and Twitter*. London: Pluto Press.

Fuchs, Christian. 2017. "From Digital Positivism and Administrative Big Data Analytics towards Critical Digital and Social Media Research!" *European Journal of Communication* 32 (1): 37–49.

Fuchs, Christian. 2008. *Internet and Society. Social Theory in the Information Age*. New York: Routledge.

Fuchs, Christian, and Jack L. Qiu. 2018. "Ferments in the Field: Introductory Reflections on the Past, Present and Future of Communication Studies". *Journal of Communication* 68 (2): 219–232.

Fuchs, Christian, and Marisol Sandoval. 2013. "The Diamond Model of Open Access Publishing: Why Policy Makers, Scholars, Universities, Libraries, Labour Unions and the Publishing World Need to Take Non-Commercial, Non-Profit Open Access Serious". *tripleC: Communication, Capitalism & Critique* 11 (2): 428–443. doi:10.31269/triplec. v11i2.502.

Fuchs, Christian, and Klaus Unterberger, eds. 2021. *The Public Service Media and Public Service Internet Manifesto*. London: University of Westminster Press.

Fung, Yiu-ming. 2009. "Philosophy in the Han Dynasty". In *Routledge Histories of World Philosophy Volume 3: History of Chinese Philosophy*, edited by Bob Mou, 269–302. Abingdon: Routledge.

Geschiere, Peter. 2021. "Dazzled by New Media: Mbembe, Tonda, and the Mystic Virutal". *African Studies Review* 64 (1): 71–85.

Giddens, Anthony. 1991. *Modernity and Self-Identity. Self and Society in the Late Modern Age*. Cambridge: Polity Press.

Giroux, Henry A. 2020. *On Critical Pedagogy*, 2nd ed. London: Bloomsbury.

Gracia, Jorge, and Manuel Vargas. 2018. "Latin American Philosophy". In *Stanford Encyclopedia of Philosophy*. https://plato.stanford.edu/entries/latin-american-philosophy/.

Grosfoguel, Ramón, Roberto Hernández, and Ernest Rosen Velásquez, eds. 2016. *Decolonizing the Westernized University*. Lanham: Lexington.

Guterman, Norbert, and Henri Lefebvre. 1936/1979. *La Conscience Mystifiée*. Paris: Le Sycomore.

Guying, Chen. 2018. *The Humanist Spirit of Daoism*. Leiden: Brill.

Habermas, Jürgen. 1992. *Postmetaphysical Thinking. Philosophical Essays*. Cambridge: The MIT Press.

Hanna, Jeffrey R. et al. 2021a. "A Qualitative Study of Bereaved Relatives' End of Life Experiences during the COVID-19 Pandemic". *Palliative Medicine* 35 (5): 843–851.

Hanna, Jeffrey R. et al. 2021b. "Health and Social Care Professionals' Experiences of Providing End of Life Care during the COVID-19 Pandemic: A Qualitative Study". *Palliative Medicine* 35 (7): 1249–1257.

Harari, Yuval Noah. 2017. *Homo Deus. A Brief History of Tomorrow*. London: Vintage.

Harari, Yuval Noah. 2011. *Sapiens. A Brief History of Humankind*. London: Vintage.

Haraway, Donna. 1991. *Simians, Cyborgs, and Women*. New York: Routledge.

Harding, Richard, and Irene J, Higginson. 2005. "Palliative Care in Sub-Saharan Africa". *The Lancet* 365 (9475): 1971–1977.

Harvey, David. 2018. "Universal Alienation". *tripleC: Communication, Capitalism & Critique* 16 (2): 424–439. doi: 10.31269/triplec.v16i2.1026.

Harvey, David. 2014. *Seventeen Contradictions and the End of Capitalism*. Oxford: Oxford University Press.

Harvey, David. 2010. *The Enigma of Capital and the Crises of Capitalism*. Oxford: Oxford University Press.

Harvey, David. 2005. *A Brief History of Neoliberalism*. Oxford: Oxford University Press.

Harvey, David. 2003. *The New Imperialism*. Oxford: Oxford University Press.

Harvey, David. 2000. *Spaces of Hope*. Edinburgh: Edinburg University Press.

Health and Social Care Committee and Science and Technology Committee. 2021. *Oral Evidence: Coronavirus: Lessons Learnt, HC 95*. Wednesday, 26 May 2021. Witness:

Dominic Cummings. https://committees.parliament.uk/oralevidence/2249/html/.

Hoad, T. F. 1996. *The Concise Oxford Dictionary of English Etymology*. Oxford: Oxford University Press.

Hofkirchner, Wolfgang. 2021. "Digital Humanism: Epistemological, Ontological and Praxiological Foundations". In *AI for Everyone? Critical Perspectives*, edited by Pieter Verdegem, 33–47. London: University of Westminster Press. doi:10.16997/book55.c.

Hofkirchner, Wolfgang. 2009. "How to Achieve a Unified Theory of Information". *tripleC* 7 (2): 357–368.

Horkheimer, Max, and Theodor W. Adorno. 2002. *Dialectic of Enlightenment. Philosophical Fragments*. Stanford: Stanford University Press.

Hou, Na. 2020. "Smart Court Campaign: China Boosts Online Litigation Services". *CGTN*, 20 April 2020. https://news.cgtn.com/news/314d444f78514464776c6d636a4e6e62684a4856/index.html.

Hou, Xiaoting et al. 2019. "Preferences for a Good Death: A Cross-Sectional Survey in Advanced Cancer Patients". *BMJ Supportive & Palliative Care*. doi:10.1136/bmjspcare-2018-001750.

Humanists International. 2020. "Governing Rules". Accessed August 4, 2021. https://docs.google.com/document/d/1evO58n_RhGJifXF-LwwnhY2AHoVhoI12PH6T3P56ZKk/edit#heading=h.c5958nhbnqen.

Illich, Ivan. 1975. *Tools for Conviviality*. Glasgow: Fontana/Collins.

Illouz, Eva. 2007. *Cold Intimacies: The Making of Emotional Capitalism*. Cambridges: Polity.

IntroBooks. 2018. *Robotics*. IntroBooks #501. Sinzig: IntroBooks.

Jacobsen, Michael Hviid, and Michael C. Kearl. 2014. "Liquid immortality – An Interview with Zygmunt Bauman". *Mortality* 19 (3): 303–317.

James, C. L. R. 1963. *Black Jacobins: Toussaint L'Ouverture and the San Domingo Revolution*. New York: Vintage.

Jameson, Frederic. 1990. "Modernism and Imperialism". In *Terry Eagleton, Frederic Jameson, and Edward W. Said: Nationalism, Colonialism, and Literature*, 43–66. Minneapolis: University of Minnesota Press.

Kearl, Michael C. 1996. "Dying Well. The Unspoken Dimension of Aging Well". *American Behavioral Scientist* 39 (3): 336–360.

Kearl, Michael C. 1989. *Ending: A Sociology of Death and Dying*. New York: Oxford University Press.

Kikule, Ekiria. 2003. "A Good Death in Uganda: Survey of Needs for Palliative Care for Terminally Ill People in Urban Areas". *British Medical Journal* 327 (7408): 192–194.

Kraidy, Marwan M. 2018. "Global Media Studies: A Critical Agenda". *Journal of Communication* 68 (2): 337–346.

Kraye, Jill. 2006. "Humanism". In *Encyclopedia of Philosophy. Volume 4: Gadamer – Just War Theory*, edited by Donald M. Borchert, 477–481. Farmington Hills: Thomson Gale.

Kumar, Sangeet, and Radhika Parameswaran. 2018. "Charting an Itinerary for Postcolonial Communication and Media Studies". *Journal of Communication* 68 (2): 347–358.

Kurzweil, Ray. 2005. *The Singularity is Near. When Humans Transcend Biology*. New York: Penguin.

Kürtüncü, Meltem, Aylin Kurt, and Nurten Arslan. 2021. "The Experiences of COVID-19 Patients in Intensive Care Units: A Qualitative Study". *Omega: The Journal of Death and Dying*. doi:10.1177/00302228211024120.

Lai, Karyn L. 2008. *An Introduction to Chinese Philosophy*. Cambridge: Cambridge University Press.

Law, Stephen. 2001. *Humanism: A Very Short Introduction*. Oxford: Oxford University Press.

Le Grange, Lesley. 2016. "Decolonising the University Curriculum". *South African Journal of Higher Education* 30 (2): 1–12.

Lefebvre, Henri. 2016. *Metaphilosophy*. London: Verso.

Lefebvre, Henri. 2003. *Key Writings*. London: Continuum.

Lefebvre, Henri. 1971a. *Au-delà du structuralisme*. Paris: Éditions Anthropos.

Lefebvre, Henri. 1971b. *Vers le cybernanthrope*. Paris: Denoël/Gonthier.

Lefebvre, Henri. 1966. *La langage et la société*. Paris: Éditions Gallimard.

Leibniz, Gottfried Wilhelm. 1703. "Explanation of Binary Arithmetic". http://www.leibniz-translations.com/binary.htm.

Ljamai, Abdelilah. 2015. "Humanistic Thought in the Islamic World of the Middle Ages". In *The Wiley Blackwell Handbook of Humanism*, edited by Andrew Copson, and A. C. Grayling, 153–169. Chicester: Wiley Blackwell.

Luik, John C. 1998. “Humanism”. In *Routledge Encyclopedia of Philosophy*, edited by Edward Craig. doi:10.4324/9780415249126-N025-1.

Luxemburg, Rosa. 1971. *Selected Political Writings of Rosa Luxemburg*. New York: Monthly Review Press.

Luxemburg, Rosa. 1916. “The Junius Pamphlet”. In *Rosa Luxemburg speaks*, by Rosa Luxemburg, 371–477. New York: Pathfinder.

Luxemburg, Rosa. 1913/2003. *The Accumulation of Capital*. London: Routledge.

Makoni, Sinfree, and Katherine A. Masters. 2021. “Decolonization and Globalization in Communication Studies”. In *Oxford Research Encyclopedia of Communication*, edited by Jon F. Nussbaum. Oxford: Oxford University Press.

Mano, Winston, and viola c. milton. 2021. “Afrokology of Media and Communication Studies. Theorising from the Margins”. In *Routledge Handbook of African Media and Communication Studies*, edited by Winston Mano, and viola c. milton, 19–42. London: Routledge.

Mariátegui, José Carlos. 2011. *An Anthology*. New York: Monthly Review Press.

Mariátegui, José Carlos. 1930. “Ethics and Socialism”. https://www.marxists.org/archive/mariateg/works/1930-ethics.htm.

Martin, Iain. 2018. “Benchmarking Widening Participation: How Should We Measure and Report Progress?” *Higher Education Policy Institute Policy Note* 6. https://www.hepi.ac.uk/wp-content/uploads/2018/04/HEPI-Policy-Note-6-Benchmarking-widening-participation-FINAL.pdf.

Marx, Karl. 1894. *Capital Volume IIII.* London: Penguin.

Marx, Karl. 1867. *Capital Volume I.* London: Penguin.

Marx, Karl. 1857/1858. *Grundrisse: Foundations of the Critique of Political Economy*. London: Penguin.

Marx, Karl. 1852. "The Eighteenth Brumaire of Louis Bonaparte". In *Marx & Engels Collected Works (MECW)*, 99–197. London: Lawrence & Wishart.

Marx, Karl. 1844a. "Contribution to the Critique of Hegel's Philosophy of Law". In *Marx & Engels Collected Works (MECW)* Volume 3, 175–187. London: Lawrence & Wishart.

Marx, Karl. 1844b. "Economic and Philosophic Manuscripts of 1844". In *Marx & Engels Collected Works (MECW)* Volume 3, 229–346. London: Lawrence & Wishart.

Marx, Karl. 1843. "On the Jewish Question". In *Marx & Engels Collected Works (MECW)* Volume 3, 146–174. London: Lawrence & Wishart.

Marx, Karl, and Friedrich Engels. 1848. "The Manifesto of the Communist Party". In *Marx & Engels Collected Works (MECW)* Volume 6, 477–519. London: Lawrence & Wishart.

Marx, Karl, and Friedrich Engels. 1845/1846. "The German Ideology". In *Marx & Engels Collected Works (MECW)* Volume 5, 19–539. London: Lawrence & Wishart.

Mason, Paul. 2019. *Clear Bright Future: A Radical Defence of the Human Being*. London: Penguin.

Mason, Paul. 2015. *PostCapitalism: A Guide to our Future*. London: Allen Lane.

Masters, Brooke. 2021. "How Britain's Private Schools Lost Their Grip on Oxbridge". *The Financial Times*, 2 July 2021.

https://www.ft.com/content/bbb7fe58-0908-4f8e-bb1a-081a42a045b7.

Mayer, Tobias. 2019. “Digitaler Humanismus. Eine Ethik für das Zeitalter der Künstlichen Intelligenz”. *Internationale Katholische Zeitschrift Communio* 15 (1): 108–110.

Mbembe, Achille. 2021. “The Universal Right to Breathe”. *Critical Inquiry* 47 (S2): S58–S62.

Mbembe, Achille. 2019. *Necropolitics*. Durham: Duke University Press.

Mbembe, Achille. 2016. “Decolonizing the University: New Directions”. *Arts and Humanities in Higher Education* 15 (1): 29–45.

Mbembe, Achille. 2015. “Decolonizing Knowledge and the Question of the Archive”. https://wiser.wits.ac.za/system/files/Achille%20Mbembe%20-%20Decolonizing%20Knowledge%20and%20the%20Question%20of%20the%20Archive.pdf.

Meinert, Carmen, ed. 2010. *Traces of Humanism in China*. Bielefeld: transcript.

Mercy Corps. 2020. The Facts: What You Need to Know About Global Hunger. Accessed May 9, 2022. https://europe.mercycorps.org/en-gb/blog/quick-facts-global-hunger.

Merrifield, Andy. 2006. *Henri Lefebvre: A Critical Introduction*. New York: Routledge.

Mies, Maria. 1986. *Patriarchy and Accumulation on a World Scale. Women in the International Division of Labour*. London: Zed Books.

milton, viola c., and Winston Mano. 2021. “Afrokology as a Transdisciplinary Approach to Media and Communication

Studies". In *Routledge Handbook of African Media and Communication Studies*, edited by Winston Mano, and viola c. milton, 256–275. London: Routledge.

Miyashita, Mitsunori et al. 2007. "Good Death in Cancer Care: A Nationwide Quantitative Study". *Annals of Oncology* 18 (6): 1090–1097.

Moravec, Hans. 1988. *Mind Children. The Future of Robot and Human Intelligence*. Cambridge: Harvard University Press.

More, Mabogo P. 2004. "Philosophy in South Africa Under and After Apartheid". In *A Companion to African Philosophy*, edited by Kwasi Wiredu, 149–160. Malden: Blackwell.

Mosco, Vincent. 2009. *The Political Economy of Communication*. London: Sage.

Murdock, Graham, and Peter Golding. 2005. "Culture, Communications and Political Economy". In *Mass Media and Society*, edited by James Curran, and Michael Gurevitch, 60–83. London: Hodder Arnold.

Mortazavi, Seyede Salehe et al. 2021. "Mourning during Corona: A Phenomenological Study of Grief Experience among Close Relatives during COVID-19 Pandemics". *Omega: The Journal of Death and Dying*. doi:10.1177/00302228211032736.

Murphy, Robin R. 2000. *Introduction to AI Robotics*. Cambridge: The MIT Press.

Musk, Elon. 2021. "Clubouse Elon Musk Interview". 7 February 2021. https://zamesin.me/clubhouse-elon-musk-interview/. Accessed August 24, 2021.

Mussato, Ariádne. 2020. *Bolsonaro: 'Brazil Must Stop Being a Country of Sissies'*. *The Brazilian Report*, 10 November 2020. https://brazilian.report/liveblog/coronavirus/2020/11/10/bolsonaro-brazil-must-stop-being-a-country-of-sissies/.

Nabudere, Dani Wadada. 2012. *Afrikology and Transdisciplinarity: A Restorative Epistemology*. Pretoria: Africa Institute for South Africa.

Nabudere, Dani Wadada. 2011. *Afrikology, Philosophy, and Wholeness: An Epistemology*. Pretoria: Africa Institute for South Africa.

Nabudere, Dani Wadada. 2006. "Towards an Afrokology of Knowledge Production and African Regeneration". *International Journal of African Renaissance Studies* 1 (1): 7–32.

Nabudere, Dan. 1977. *The Political Economy of Imperialism*. London: Zed.

Namisango, Eva, Elly Katabira, Charles Karamagi, and Peter Baguma. 2007. "Validation of the Missoula-Vitas Quality-of-Life Index among Patients with Advanced AIDS in Urban Kampala, Uganda". *Journal of Pain and Symptom Management* 33 (2): 189–202.

Nida-Rümelin, Julian, and Nathalie Weidenfeld. 2018. *Digitaler Humanismus. Eine Ethik für das Zeitalter der Künstlichen Intelligenz*. Munich: Piper.

Noble, David F. 1995. *Progress without People. New Technology, Unemployment, and the Message of Resistance*. Toronto: Between the Lines.

Norman, Richard. 2004. *On Humanism*. London: Routledge.

Nuccetelli, Susana. 2020. *An Introduction to Latin American Philosophy*. Cambridge: Cambridge University Press.

Nyamnjoh, Francis B. 2020. *Decolonising the Academy. A Case for Convivial Scholarship*. Basel: Baseler Afrika Bibliographien.

Nyamnjoh, Francis B. 2017. "Incompleteness: Frontier Africa and the Currency of Conviviality". *Journal of Asian and African Studies* 52 (3): 253–270.

Nyamnjoh, Francis B. 2002. "'A Child is One Person's Only in the Womb': Domestication, Agency and Subjectivity in the Cameroonian Grassfields". In *Postcolonial Subjectivities in Africa*, edited by Richard Werbner, 111–138. London: Zed Books.

Ngũgĩ wa Thiong'o. 1986. *Decolonising the Mind*. Nairobi: Heinemann Kenya.

Nkrumah, Kwame. 1965. *Neo-Colonialism*. New York: International Publishers.

Online Etymology Dictionary. 2021. "convivial (adj.)". Accessed July 16, 2021. https://www.etymonline.com/word/convivial#etymonline_v_18319.

Oxfam. 2021. "The Hunger Virus Multiplies". Oxfam Media Briefing, 9 July 2021. https://oi-files-d8-prod.s3.eu-west-2.amazonaws.com/s3fs-public/2021-07/The%20Hunger%20Virus%202.0_media%20brief_EN.pdf.

Patterson, Orlando. 1982. *Slavery and Social Death. A Comparative Study*. Cambridge, MA: Harvard University Press.

Pentaris, Panagiotis, and Kate Woodthorpe. 2022. "Familiarity With Death". In *Death, Grief and Loss in the Context of COVID-19*, edited by Panagiotis Pentaris, 17–28. London: Routledge.

Piketty, Thomas. 2014. *Capital in the Twenty-First Century*. Cambridge: Belknap Press.

Pitanupong, Jarurin, and Sahawit Janmanee. 2021. "End-of-Life Care Preferences among Cancer Patients in Southern Thailand: A University Hospital-Based Cross-Sectional Analysis". *BMC Palliative Care* 20 (90). doi:10.1186/s12904-021-00775-6.

Plaul, Constantin. 2019. "Digitaler Humanismus. Eine Ethik für das Zeitalter der Künstlichen Intelligenz". *Zeitschrift für Evangelische Ethik* 63 (3): 234–235.

Porter, Theodor M. 2018. *Digital Humanism* 21 (4): 369–373.

Postone, Moishe. 2003. "The Holocaust and the Trajectory of the Twentieth Century". In *Catastrophe and Meaning: The Holocaust and the Twentieth Century*, edited by Moishe Postone and Eric Santner, 81–114. Chicago: University of Chicago Press.

Public Service Media and Public Service Internet Manifesto. 2021. "The Public Service Media and Public Service Internet Manifesto". http://bit.ly/psmmanifesto, https://archive.org/details/@public_service_media_and_public_service_internet_manifesto.

Querejazu, Amaya. 2016. "Encountering the Pluriverse: Looking for Alternatives in other Worlds". *Revista Brasileira de Política Internacional* 59 (2). doi:10.1590/0034-7329201600207.

Ramose, Mogobe B. 2003. "Globalization and Ubuntu". In *The African Philosophy Reader*, edited by Pieter H. Coetzee, and Abraham P. J. Roux, 626–649, 2nd ed. New York: Routledge.

Rao, K. Narayana. 2017. "Indian Thought of Humanism: Answer for Cheerful Human Life". *Global Journal for Research Analysis* 6 (9): 64–66.

Rifkin, Jeremy. 1995. *The End of Work. The Decline of the Global Labor Force and the Dawn of the Post-Market Era.* New York: Tarcher/Putnam.

Rodríguez-Ortega, Nuria. 2018. "Five Central Concepts to Think of Digital Humanities as a New Digital Humanism Project". *Artnodes* 22: 1–6.

Roy, Arundhati. 2021. "'We Are Witnessing a Crime Against Humanity': Arundhati Roy on India's Covid Catastrophe". *The Guardian*, 28 April 2021. https://www.theguardian.com/news/2021/apr/28/crime-against-humanity-arundhati-roy-india-covid-catastrophe.

Saha, Subir Kuma. 2014. *Introduction to Robotics*, 2nd ed. New Delhi: McGraw-Hill.

Said, Edward W. 2003. *Orientalism*. London: Penguin.

Sandsdalen, Tuva, Reidun Hov, Sevald Høye, Ingrid Rystedt, and Bodil Wilde-Larsson. 2015. "Patients' Preferences in Palliative Care: A Systematic Mixed Studies Review". *Palliative Medicine* 29 (5): 399–419.

Santos, Boaventura de Sousa. 2019. "Decolonizing the University". In *Knowledges Born in Struggle*, edited by Boaventura de Sousa Santos, and Maria Paula Meneses, 219–239. New York: Routledge.

Santos, Boaventura de Sousa. 2018. *The End of the Cognitive Empire. The Coming of Age of Epistemologies of the South.* Durham: Duke University Press.

Santos, Boaventura de Sousa. 2017. *Decolonising the University. The Challenge of Deep Cognitive Justice.* Newcastle upon Tyne: Cambridge Scholars.

Santos, Boaventura de Sousa. 2016. *Epistemologies of the South. Justice Against Epistemicide.* Abingdon: Routledge.

Sartre, Jean-Paul. 1964/2001. *Colonialism and Neocolonialism.* London: Routledge.

Sartre, Jean-Paul. 1963. "Preface". In *Frantz Fanon: The Wretched of the Earth*, 7–31. New York: Grove Press.

Searle, John. 1990. "Is the Brain's Mind a Computer Program". *Science* 262 (1): 26–31.

Selman, Lucy E. et al. 2021. "Sadness, Despair and Anger When A Patient Dies Alone from COVID-19: A Thematic Content Analysis of Twitter Data from Bereaved Family Members and Friends". *Palliative Medicine* 35 (7): 1267–1276.

Selman, Lucy E. et al. 2011. "Quality of Life among Patients Receiving Palliative Care in South Africa and Uganda: A Multi-Centred Study". *Health and Quality of Life Outcomes* 9 (21). doi:10.1186/1477-7525-9-21.

Shi, Changqing, Tani Sourdin, and Bin Li. 2021. "The Smart Court – A New Pathway to Justice in China?" *International Journal for Court Administration* 12 (1). doi:10.36745/ijca.367.

Shields, Rob. 1999. *Lefebvre, Love and Struggle. Spatial Dialectics.* London: Routledge.

Shome, Raka. 2016. "When Postcolonial Studies Meets Media Studies". *Critical Studies in Media Communication* 33 (3): 245–263.

Slater, Joanna, and Niha Masih. 2021. "In India's Surge, a Religious Gathering Attended by Millions Helped the Virus Spread". *The Washington Post*, 8 May 2021. https://www.washingtonpost.com/world/2021/05/08/india-coronavirus-kumbh-mela/.

Soper, Kate. 2005. "Humanism". In *The Concise Encyclopedia of Western Philosophy*, edited by Jonathan Rée, and J. O. Urmson, 167–168, 3rd ed. Abingdon: Routledge.

Sparks, Colin. 2018. "Changing Concepts for a Changing World". *Journal of Communication* 68 (2): 390–398.

Srnicek, Nick, and Alex Williams. 2015. *Inventing the Future. Postcapitalism and a World without Work*, ebook ed. London: Verso.

Stalin, Joseph. 1928. "Industrialisation of the Country and the Right Deviation in the C.P.S.U. (B)". In *Stalin Works* Volume 11, 255–302. Moscow: Foreign Languages Publishing House.

State Council of the People's Republic of China. 2017. "A Next Generation Artificial Intelligence Development Plan". Accessed June 22, 2021. https://www.airuniversity.af.edu/Portals/10/CASI/documents/Translations/2021-03-02%20China's%20New%20Generation%20Artificial%20Intelligence%20Development%20Plan-%202017.pdf?ver=N2TtRVNODYyWR0yGHuK_cA%3d%3d.

Steinhauser, Karen E. et al. 2000. "Factors Considered Important at the End of Life by Patients, Family, Physicians, and Other Care Providers". *JAMA* 284 (19): 2476–2482.

Suzuki, Daisetz Teitaro, Erich Fromm, and Richard De Martino. 1970. *Zen Buddhism & Psychoanalysis*. New York: Harper & Row.

Suzuki, Daisetz Teitaro. 2015. "On Satori – The Revelation of a New Truth in Zen Buddhism". In *Selected Works of D. T. Suzuki. Volume I: Zen*, edited by Richard M. Jaffe, 14–38. Oakland: University of California Press.

Terec-Vlad, Loredana, and Daniel Terec-Vlad. 2014. "About the Evolution of the Human Species: Human Robots and Human Enhancement". 2014. *Postmodern Openings* 5 (3): 67–75.

Thomas, Mike. 2019. "The Future of AI: How Artificial Intelligence Will Change the World". *Builtin.com*, 8 June 2019. https://builtin.com/artificial-intelligence/artificial-intelligence-future.

Thussu, Daya. 2009. *Internationalizing Media Studies*. London: Routledge.

Tillich, Paul. 1952. *Protestantische Vision*. Stuttgart: Ring Verlag.

Trovato, Gabriele. et al. 2021. "Religion and Robots: Towards the Synthesis of Two Extremes". *International Journal of Social Robotics* 13 (4): 539–556.

Tu, Weiming. 2003. "Confucianism: Humanism and the Enlightenment". In *Encyclopedia of Chinese Philosophy*, edited by Antonio S. Cua, 89–96. New York: Routledge.

UNCTAD (United Nations Conference on Trade and Development). 2020. *Trade and Development Report 2020*. New York: United Nations Publications.

UNCTAD (United Nations Conference on Trade and Development). 2019. *Digital Economy Report 2019*. New York: United Nations Publications.

United Nations. 2020. *Human Development Report 2020*. New York: United Nations Development Programme.

Waisbord, Silvio, and Claudia Mellado. 2014. "De-Westernizing Communication Studies: A Reassessment". *Communication Theory* 24 (4): 361–372.

Wallace, Rob. 2020. *Dead Epidemiologists. On the Origins of COVID-19*. New York: Monthly Review Press.

Wallerstein, Immanuel. 2004. *World-Systems Analysis. An Introduction*. Durham: Duke University Press.

Walter, Tony. 2020. *Death in the Modern World*. London: Sage.

Walter, Tony. 2003. "Historical and Cultural Variants on the Good Death". *British Medical Journal* 327 (7408): 218–220.

Walter, Tony, Rachid Hourizi, Wendy Moncur, and Stacey Pitsillides. 2011. *Omega: The Journal of Death and Dying* 64 (4): 275–302.

Wang, Georgette, ed. 2011. *De-Westernizing Communication Research: Altering Questions and Changing Frameworks*. Abingdon: Routledge.

Wang, Ruoshui. 1997. "My Marxist Outlook". *Contemporary Chinese Thought* 29 (1): 35–96.

Wang, Ruoshui. 1984a. "Man is the Starting Point of Marxism". *China Report* 20 (3): 36–45.

Wang, Ruoshui. 1984b. "On the Problem of Alienation". *China Report* 20 (3): 25–35.

Weale, Sally, Richard Adams, and Helena Bengtsson. 2017. "Oxbridge Becoming Less Diverse as Richest Gain 80% of Offers". *The Guardian*, 19 October 2017. https://www.theguardian.com/education/2017/oct/19/oxbridge-becoming-less-diverse-as-richest-gain-80-of-offers.

Weizenbaum, Joseph. 1976. *Computer Power and Human Reason. From Judgment to Calculation*. New York: W. H. Freeman and Company.

White House. 2020. "Artificial Intelligence for the American People". Accessed June 22, 2021. https://trumpwhitehouse.archives.gov/ai/.

Widdau, Christoph Sebastian. 2019. "Digitaler Humanismus. Eine Ethik für das Zeitalter der Künstlichen Intelligenz". *Zeitschrift für Philosophische Forschung* 72 (2): 307–310.

Willems, Wendy. 2014. "Provincializing Hegemonic Histories of Media and Communication Studies: Toward a Genealogy of Epistemic Resistance in Africa". *Communication Theory* 24 (4): 415–434.

Willems, Wendy, and Winston Mano. 2016. "Decolonizing and Provincializing Audience and Internet Studies: Contextual Approaches from African Vantage Points". In *Everyday Media Culture in Africa: Audiences and Users*, eds. Wendy Willems, and Winston Mano, 1–26. London: Routledge.

Winfield, Alan. 2012. *Robotics. A Very Short Introduction*. Oxford: Oxford University Press.

Wiredu, Kwasi. 1996. *Cultural Universals and Particulars. An African Perspective*. Bloomington: Indiana University Press.

Wiredu, Kwasi. 1995. "Are There Cultural Universals?" *The Monist* 78 (1): 52–64.

Xinhua. 2019a. "Beijing Internet Court Launches AI Judge". *XinhuaNet*, 28 June 2019. http://www.chinadaily.com.cn/a/201906/28/WS5d156cada3103dbf1432ac74.html.

Xinhua. 2019b. "Chinese Courts to Embrace AI". XinhuaNet, 11 March 2019. http://www.xinhuanet.com/english/2019-03/11/c_137886496.htm.

Žižek, Slavoj. 2021. "Blade Runner 2049: A View of Post-Human Capitalism". In *Lacanian Perspectives on Blade Runner 2049*, edited by Calum Neill, 41–51. Cham: Palgrave Macmillan.

Žižek, Slavoj. 2020. *Hegel in a Wired Brain*. London: Bloomsbury Academic.

Žižek, Slavoj. 2018. *Like a Thief in Broad Daylight: Power in the Era of Post-Human Capitalism*. London: Allen Lane.

Žižek, Slavoj. 2017. *Incontinence of the Void. Economico-Philosophical Spandrels*. Cambridge: The MIT Press.

Žižek, Slavoj. 2016. *Disparities*. London: Bloomsbury Academic.

INDEX